FRIENDS
of
His Presence

ALEJANDRO ARIAS

FIRST EDITION

ISBN: 978-0-9970518-8-9

Library of Congress Control Number: 2016938451

Published by

P.O. Box 2839, Apopka, FL 32703

Printed in the United States of America

Contents

Endorsements

This book starts as if someone had pushed you in a river. There is no meandering as Alejandro brings you right to the secrets of a friendship with God. Alejandro writes from a long steady experience of living in his Friend's presence. The first time Alejandro visited us in Medellin, Colombia, he asked to use my office for prayer. I asked him if I could pray with him, but I didn't pray so much as watch him talk, worship and listen to his Friend. I thought my prayer life was vanilla while Alejandro's had all the flavors of Ben & Jerry. That day spurred me into a deeper friendship with Jesus, and this book will do the same for you.

— Pastor Andrew McMillan
Comunidad Cristiana de Fe
Medellin, Colombia

Nothing is more rewarding than engaging with someone who is deeply in love with you and is able to open up your potential, bringing out the best in you, making you fully alive. That's exactly what Alejandro has done. In his newest book he reveals God, who deeply loves you, and is passionate and able to transform your life into the wonder He created you for. Jesus' statement in Matthew saying, "Seek you first the kingdom of God and His righteousness and all these things will be added to you," becomes the underlying theme of Alex's words to us as he inspires us to a full and rich friendship with Jesus Christ. Get ready to be changed!

— Monte Knudsen, Pastor
Faith Christian Outreach Church
Mount Pleasant, IA

Alejandro is a burning revivalist igniting a generation! This book will give you keys to becoming a catalyst to move with the heart of Jesus to see His power and transformation come to your family, your community and the nations!

— Steven Springer,
Senior Apostolic Leader of Global Presence
Madison WI, USA.

Like one who has discovered the cure for an incurable disease that has for ages dwarfed, maimed and destroyed many, Brother Alejandro Arias in *Friends of His Presence* is passionately imploring us all to move in and be drenched with the Father's Glory so we can go demonstrate the majesty of His power in this untoward generation.

— Pastor Festus Nsoha,
Veteran Missionary and Senior Pastor Oasis Church
Prague, Czech Republic

Outstanding reading. Inspirational, insightful and will increase your understanding of who God is and stir your faith to follow Him all the way. Well done, Alejandro!

— Pastor Stewart Moncrieff,
Freshwater Church,
Cairns QLD Australia

Chapter 1

Friends of God

Jesus said,

"You are my friends if you do what I command you. I no longer call you servants, because a servant does not know his master's business. Instead, I have called you friends, for everything that I have learned from my Father I have made known to you." (John 15:14,15)

Jesus was referring to the servants of God not having the same level of relationship when compared to those who are friends of God.

When we examine verse 14, Jesus teaches us that the price of being friends of God's presence is obedience to Christ's Word. Let's remember that we can't please God without faith in our hearts (Hebrews 11:6); also faith is enlarged by obedience. For this reason, God was pleased with Abraham, and what's more, God called him "friend," as mentioned in James 2:23:

"And the Scripture was fulfilled that says, 'Abraham believed God, and it was credited to him as righteousness,' and he was called God's friend."

This truth described in Scripture was fulfilled when Abraham believed God; it was credited to him as righteousness, and he was called a friend of God.

Abraham was called a "Friend of God," because his faith in God was counted as righteousness and he obeyed the voice of the Lord. God asked Abraham for the most precious thing in his life to test his faith. It's precisely for this reason that God honored Abraham by calling him the father of faith. I can picture Abraham on his way to the land of Moriah in Jerusalem. Abraham took his son by the hand and walked together toward Mt. Moriah, as narrated in Genesis 22:2-19. Abraham had no uncertainty in his heart, hearing the still yet great voice of his friend that woke him up early in the morning as only God can do. This particular time it was to ask Abraham for his most beloved; his only son, as described in verse 2.

Abraham pleased God once again by being loyal to His friend. He arose early and prepared all for the sacrifice. Since he did not have the animal offering, his son questioned him curiously and persistently, "Daddy, where is the goat for the sacrifice?" His father probably responded with a nervous smile, "God will provide, son." Even though his heart hid a deep pain for his child, he preferred to obey God than to be driven by his emotions. We all know the end of this terrifying yet amazing act of faith. God, in the end, provided a goat and Isaac's life was spared. It was as if God was looking at what Abraham was going through, looking ahead to the day when His Son was going to be given as an offering to save all mankind.

We see a contrast here when the Father was pained to see His Son Jesus on the cross of Calvary just as Abraham was hurting deeply when he had to put his son on the altar. Two different stories and yet both produced a great outcome in the spiritual realm. Jesus was obedient, and as the Bible tells us, He was led as a sheep to the slaughter. We see the Roman authorities lifting up the Messiah on the cross and the Pharisees blaspheming Him. However, the same ones that crucified Him were also the witnesses on the third day when Jesus was resurrected and fulfilled the dream of His Father. Jesus alone was the only man to have gained reconciliation for all humanity with the presence of God, hence providing a path for all of us to become His friend. This truth is expanded as we recall what the Word states in Romans 3:23-24:

> "For all have sinned and fallen short of the glory of God, and are justified freely by his grace through the redemption that came by Christ Jesus."

For generations the Father was separated from that which He loved most: His creation. Notwithstanding, during various decades the Father communicated his precepts to chosen men; those called to be His friends. As we can see repeatedly in the Scriptures, God would only talk to the prophets, the priests and sometimes the kings. If we go deeper and study this revelation, we can see that the veil that separated the Holy Place from the Holy of Holies in the Tabernacle of Moses was the same veil that separated human beings from His presence. However when Christ died, as the Bible says, there was a great earthquake and the veil was torn apart. This is very symbolic because, from that day, we were given freedom to come and go into His presence anytime our hearts desire. That said, He doesn't just talk to prophets or people in ministry nowadays but anyone who has an open ear and is hungry for the greatness of His glory!

In that moment, when Abraham had prepared the altar and all was ready for him to take his son and lay him down upon the altar, I can imagine how the heavens suddenly became quiet, as the angels looked towards the earth and curiously observed the man of faith. Imagine the agony and overwhelming pain Abraham was enduring when he lifted his knife and perhaps heard the words of his son saying, "Dad what are you doing?" as Abraham laid his son on that rocky altar. There was nothing around them, but the wilderness of Mt. Moriah. Just in that instant, when Abraham intended to lift the knife and offer the covenant offering, God's silence ceased and immediately a powerful voice rang out from the throne of glory; the Father himself ordered the angels to stop him. We can envision the scene of this man of God from our human perspective. In the middle of the desert, with beads of sweat running down his cheeks, merging with tears in the midst of his memories, and afflicted because of the breaking of his heart into a thousand pieces, when he suddenly heard a voice from heaven call him by name saying,

> "Do not lay a hand on the boy, do not do anything to him. Now I know that you fear God, because you have not withheld from me your son, your only son." (Genesis 22:12)

Can you imagine this moment in the life of the patriarch

– how God responded saying that He now knew that Abraham feared God because he had not denied what had been asked of him? (Genesis 22:9-12)

Chapter 2

The Valiant of God

God is calling for a generation that fears Him; that honors Him. A generation that would listen to the King's heartbeat that pulses for the salvation of souls. Only God's friends can hear the heartbeat of Jesus as they walk into His chambers with thanksgiving. Jesus said in Matthew 11:12,

> "...the kingdom of heaven suffers violence, and the violent take it by force."

Therefore, only brave people who are willing to lay down their life for the sake of others may become really close friends. Having said that, I want to clarify that God's desire is that anyone can become His friend. There is a very clear difference between a son and a friend. When we accept Christ, we become His children but not necessarily His friends. Friendship is something that speaks volumes of the person's loyalty and integrity. It is God's ultimate desire that when His heart beats, your heart would beat also, as we see in the Bible narration of King David's three most intimate friends. When his mighty men heard the petition, he cried out,

> "Oh, that someone would get me a drink of water
> from the well near the gate of Bethlehem!"
>
> (2 Samuel 23:15)

These men did not doubt or hesitate in their hearts if they were to satisfy their king's desire. Despite the fact that the Philistines guarded the well, they ran and organized the plot. With my limited imagination, I wonder how this all played out; maybe one with a sword, another with a bucket and rope to draw the water, and the third one fighting against the Philistines. This was no easy task, as they had to fight the enemies and perhaps get hurt in the process. In fact, when they returned to the king carrying the water, he refused to drink it, replying to them,

> "Is this not the blood of the men who went at the
> risk of their lives?" (2 Samuel 23:17)

He immediately poured out the water as an offering to God. These men were not fickle-hearted but rather they showed a great amount of courageousness and faithfulness to their king. God yearns to see such friends in His courts, those who will know and execute His plans. Can you imagine the water changing into blood? Those men fought to satisfy the king's request and present it before him. Certainly the Father is seeking for a generation of friends that fight for their cities, families and for their nations.

Have you ever heard the vow that is often said in a wedding ceremony, "I promise I will be faithful in good times but also in bad times." Well, the very truth of this vow is formed in a deep friendship of two individuals who love each other and are willing to stick with each other in good or bad times. In fact, I dare say that a good marriage is really a great friendship. That's why it is so wise and advisable for any couple to have a time of courting before they enter into the covenant of marriage. It is the same with our God; He is looking for friends who are willing to leave everything behind for His purpose, who will be faithful to His presence on good and bad days. I know that some of you may be thinking that this is easier said than done. But in order to be part of the bride, we must form a deep friendship with our beloved Savior! That is the key to have access into His heart on a daily basis. Many can pray and ask for mercy but only a few may enter into His chambers. Many of you may be pondering, so what is the secret to being His friend: the answer is faithfulness and valiancy. This is the hour my friend to take authority as a friend of God and rise up. Be sufficient only in His Word, obey God's design for your life and acknowledge today that the heart of Jesus beats for souls.

Those who, no matter what the price is about, will be willing to do whatever it takes and will try to execute God's plan with no conditions. A generation that unconditionally serves God with fervent passion and who are willing to go the extra mile are those who will make the difference in this 'desperate for change' society we live in.

As the mighty men of King David, who didn't spare their lives and went into the mouth of the lion, so to speak, fought valiantly until they got the water from the well and ran back to the cave of Adullam, as the Scriptures says in 2 Samuel 23:14-16. God wants to raise a generation of people that are walking in the power of His Word and therefore brave enough to conquer the stolen land and recover the lost treasures. This is not a mandate for the faint of heart but for people who are hungry to have a great friendship with the King of kings and therefore know clearly the desires of His heart. Would you be one of those mighty men God is looking for? This delegation Jesus dreams of must have the spirit of an eagle and fly above the heights like eagles do. One of the things that I most admire about eagles is that when there is a storm, they fly higher in order to rise above the tempest. In this same manner, it is time for the mighty men and women of God to arise and commence the most glorious flight of their lives; to fulfill the Father's will, flying above their problems and circumstances. The prophet Isaiah refers to this allegory of the eagle when he said,

> "Those who hope in the Lord will renew their strength. They will soar on wings as eagles, they will run and not grow weary, and they will walk and not grow faint." (Isaiah 40:31)

Chapter 3

Worshipers in Spirit and in Truth

Jesus once said when his disciples approached Him and asked Him about prayer, that His Father was seeking for worshipers who worship in spirit and in truth. I remember once reading that passage and feeling somewhat heartbroken and baffled wondering why the Lord Jesus said that He was still looking for worshipers in spirit and in truth, and then the answer came to me as if God was reading my thoughts and He whispered to my ears and said, "My son, many are churchgoers but few are worshipers." Then I understood the importance of what it is to be a worshiper and the clear difference between a church member and a worshiper. Many people say that they worship at such and such a church and what they really mean is that they attend church. Many raise their hands, jump up and down, give their offerings and tithes but yet don't quite make it all the way to the Holy of Holies or the most intimate place, where the Father desires His people to come for fresh manna from heaven.

As many of you know God works in patterns and these patterns are often revealed to prophets and common men to bring them down to earth and make them a reality. Before there was ever a temple on earth, there was one in heaven as it is explained to us in Revelation 8:1-4. Here we read about the activities in the temple in Heaven which reflects Old Testament worship. Before there was dance, worship, flags, praise instruments and other things, there was a revelation of these tools of worship and they were implemented in our worship practice on earth. What I am trying to say is that someone must have seen a vision or had a dream before these instruments came about. Most people that have had visions of heaven, including myself, have seen these amazing instruments which were being used in heavenly worship also being replicated and used on earth. So my point is that the tabernacle used in Moses time, the temple Solomon built and the temple in Jesus day were patterned after the temple that is in heaven. The most intricate architectural pattern ever given to men was the Ark of the Covenant and Noah's ark. Both were magnificently built and perfect right down to the last piece of wood. However, both these divinely engineered projects were designed to speak of the glory and greatness of our God! When we talk about worship we are actually speaking of one of the most renown and oldest patterns ever revealed to men. God breathed His breath upon music and everything that is created has some sort of sound in it. The right combination of sounds makes a perfect and pleasant melody. Recently NASA discovered that there is a unique sound that every planet makes when listened to through special technology, and what is fascinating is that the sound our planet earth makes is the one of a mother giving birth.

The earth is waiting for the manifestation of the children of God just as mentioned in the Scriptures:

"For the earnest expectation of the creature waiteth
for the manifestation of the sons of God."
(Romans 8:19 KJV)

Worship did not originate on earth as God had the original orchestra playing for HIM in heaven. You want to know how powerful worship is? Let's talk about the one who was thrown out of heaven because of pride but also because he wanted the worship God only deserves. That's right, Lucifer had an ego trip and his pride reached to a limit that God himself had to expel the most beautiful angel He had created and the one who was in charge of leading the others in worship. What I am saying is that Lucifer, "Satan," knows how powerful worship is and that is why he was kicked out of heaven. (See Ezekiel 28:16-17) He has been trying for generations and generations to corrupt the most wonderful and powerful resource that was meant for our Father God alone!

Ever since that event took place there has been a battle on between the enemy and man. What many of us don't realize is that the enemy is constantly battling against us because he knows that we are God's most precious creation. I want you to realize today the enemy knows what God deeply desires and is moved by "worship" and that's the reason he rebelled and deceived a third of the angels, wanting to create his own empire and be worshiped by them. God longs for worshipers in spirit and truth and that's the reason why there are angels up there singing and playing instruments 24/7. However, when the worship sound comes from earth and HIS creation adore Him, He literally stops every instrument and singing angel just to hear His creation's melody as we all stand from every corner of this world and give Him praise. In fact, the Bible says that we were created to worship, and if so, then there is great importance in the exercise and act of worship. It is very relevant in heaven and so it should be on earth. God longs to hear the worship of His worshipers.

Being a worshiper is the secret to access heaven

To illustrate the relevance of being a worshiper, one of the great examples of devotion and character for me is the life of the young shepherd David. He would often rise at the first rays of the dawn to sit in the meadows before the sea of Galilee, and with harp in hand, begin to delight himself in God's glory. He was a true worshiper and a general who marked the history of his time. But what was his secret? What was the key to his promotion from shepherd to the king of Israel? Truly it was the psalmist's passion that drove him to deeply know the God of his ancestors, and his brave heart that brought him to the battleground where he defeated the giant Goliath by the Spirit of God. The Word of God teaches us that when an evil spirit was tormenting King Saul, he was often aggravated and his servants had to bring him a harpist who could play and bring relief to the king's life. In that dialogue between the servants and Saul, one of them arose, saying,

> "Lord King, I have seen a son of Jesse of Bethlehem
> who knows how to play the harp. He is a brave man

and a warrior. He speaks well and is a fine-looking man. And the Lord is with him." (1 Samuel 16:18)

King Saul then sent to Jesse to ask for his son David. If we contemplate these characteristics mentioned, we see a profound surrender and communion on David's part with his best friend, the God of Israel.

His worship example must be a model for all of us as believers. His devotion and his intense prayer life was David's number one weapon in his times of need, brokenness, failure, and even defeat. He never stopped giving worship, and at the end, we can see that despite King David's eventful reign, God never forsook him and even though David failed on a couple of accounts, God redeemed David and put his name up on a really special list. God called him "A man after His own heart."

Being a worshiper is to be one's lifestyle in their devotion and constant pursuit of God. Worshipers will never get tired of seeking HIM and they are never content with your typical 30 minutes praise time, five minutes offering message and five points message – they will want more than that! They go beyond their Sunday service experience to a new level of profoundness and intimacy with the Creator of all sounds ever given to men! Music, arts, and poetry were created in heaven before they were given to men. As we read the book of Psalms, we can see that David was a great poet. Solomon was quite the same and we can talk about many prophets who, on various occasions, used worship, sound instruments and other tools to communicate a message or bring great victories about!

Chapter 4

Sonship, the Key for Your Identity

Psalmist David was a passionate singer and shepherd. During his journey in the meadows of Bethlehem as the little boy tending the sheep, his passion grew to such an extent that he was moved to write many of the worship psalms we see in the Scriptures today. David had a family and a father. In fact, he did not grow up feeling like an orphan because he knew his father and had fellowship with him. One application we can see here is that every worshiper must be first a son and therefore have a spiritual covering upon their life. You have to know that you are a son of God in order that the world would see God in you. Let's remember that before being a servant or a leader, we are His children.

It is necessary that we as God's people know our heavenly Father, and that we may dwell in His glory and eat at the table served in the most holy place as children of the household, not as visitors. When I use the term "visitor" I am referring to a regrettable reality with many Christians who draw near to the presence of God as visitors, saying a very formal prayer, reading the Bible perhaps for some fifteen minutes and making their devotional time all about structure. By this I do not mean to say that having devotion in such a way is wrong, rather that it is sad when there is the absence of a profound relationship between the Creator and His creation. A visitor will never have the same rights and privileges as sons and daughters have. In fact, when a visitor speaks out of term and steps out of boundary, there is the risk that such a visitor may never be invited again. A visitor does not have the same freedom to walk around the house and do as he pleases, as this is not his house. Nonetheless, there is a very clear mark which differentiates one relationship from the other, and that is closeness and freedom. A son will have more rights, benefits, privileges, and responsibilities as opposed to what is expected from a guest. It is heart breaking when you see some church folks that have been going to church for years and yet they are not behaving as sons and daughters as they are not expressing true freedom during their worship time. Many of you may say, wait a second, not everyone has to worship the Lord the same way. Is there a parameter to measure if I am behaving as a son or as a visitor? Well my friend, I am not writing this to ostracize the way you worship but rather to teach you that there is a better way of worship and that is having a close relationship with your heavenly Father. I am not dictating how you do that or what the expression of your worship is going to be like, but one thing I can assure you is, that if you follow David's example in the way he worshiped, your prayer life will be revolutionized and thus your faith will become stronger!

Perhaps this is the perfect moment for you to speak with

your Father as a son/daughter, and that you may leave behind all guilt and enter into your Father's house with freedom and thanksgiving. I assure you that if you do this after reading this chapter your life will be transformed.

God does not want to give you an audience with Him; He wants to commune with you as His child. Remember that Jesus said,

> "But as many as received Him, to them He gave the right to become children of God, to those who believe in His name." (John 1:12)

Being a true son of God is knowing who your Father is. Many believers attend revival meetings to have a touch from God and get a prophetic word from the known prophet or visiting speaker coming to their town. The saddest reality is that many are satisfied with one prayer or one meeting a week and they go home and live off that, rather than discovering their true identity as a son and coming into the presence of the Father on a daily basis. One of the greatest benefits of grace is that we may access His throne every day if we please to and have an encounter with our heavenly Daddy. True friends of God are true sons of God as this concept goes hand in hand. As a child of God, it is your privilege and heaven given right to eat the bread of the children and therefore delight in the glory of His presence.

How can we put up barriers against this love which surpasses all understanding? This is the time for you to experience the true Father and son relationship. Remembering that every day our Father is always waiting for us, and that He has prepared the biggest banquet in the most Holy Place, so that you can come and spend time with HIM.

Chapter 5

God's Warriors

It is a sunny day as the young David pastures his father's sheep as always. Then suddenly he hears the voice of an old man calling him – to his surprise it is his father's voice. David runs through the meadows to him, who says, "David, it's lunch time. Go to the battle camp where your brothers are and take them these cheeses, milk and cakes." David nods and agrees to go. He immediately takes the provisions and starts out for the camp. Along the way he suddenly hears loud voices, one in particular louder and more irritating than the others.

David decides to rest a moment, exhausted from the long walk and hears the voices break the silence once again, this time with words discernable to the little shepherd. He hears the voice of the nation's enemy shouting, "Ha! Who will dare to defeat me?" followed by great insults to the people of Israel. In this time there lived giants in the land, and this one was also a Philistine. The youth runs until he arrives at the camp, flushed from his race, and lifts his gaze to glance at the giant measuring more than two meters in stature. David looks at the enemy army, his warrior blood beginning to course through his veins, but he continues on until reaching where his brothers are to give them their provisions. Although they question why David came and the reason for their father sending him, when David is ordered to go, he does not want to leave. As he was walking around the camp back and forth, irritated by this giant's threats, David suddenly asks the key question that will bring him before the king. David asks the same question twice, but the soldiers do not understand why he asks it. They immediately make it known to the king however, who allows David to come before him. To the king's surprise, the same boy who entered was the same one who had played the harp when the evil spirit tormented him. King Saul exclaims, saying, "David, what are you doing here!"

Whereupon the youth responds, "I have felt the living zeal of Jehovah and I believe that today God will give this Philistine into my hand, as he also did with the lion and the bear. Who does this giant believe he is to terrorize the people of the God of Israel?"

The king, although impressed by all of David's victories, replies, "But David, you are a boy and this is a man who has been a warrior since his youth."

David answers him, "God has spoken to me."

Without knowing how to convince him, Saul ends up saying, "Very well David, may God be with you," and removes all his own royal armor, which is certainly heavy. Evidently, David feels burdened by the total weight of the load, and so decides not to use the armor but rather trust in someone superior. David goes out from the presence of the king, running as any boy in the direction of a brook. His brothers see him from a distance and ask themselves what mischief the boy could be about to do. It happens that David knows that the perfect place to find the victory is in the stream of God's presence. Thus trusting, he takes some pebbles from the riverbed and sets out to the battlefield. Suddenly he is in front of thousands of enemy soldiers and allies of that nation, whom look at him from afar. At that moment, some begin to laugh whilst others question what the little boy is going to do…eventually silence descends on the multitude. The Bible teaches us that in this instant the Philistine gives voice to threats and blasphemies and as he looks at David, he "despises him". The Philistine sees David as a youth bestowed with beauty and is filled with loathing for him.

However minutes later, this young David is a complete soldier at the battle line. In this crucial moment, the eyes of the multitude are on David. He takes the stone and sling. The whole audience follows the stone with their gaze as it crosses the battlefield, but something powerful happens just at the moment it is launched. The power of God is infused into the stone and impacts the giant's forehead. Dizzy and weak, the giant sways and falls to the ground. It is when the soldiers break the silence again and all Israel celebrates the victory that David, unsatisfied with the fall, takes the giant's sword and cuts off his head. (This is my paraphrase of the story of David and Goliath found in 1 Samuel 17.)

Can you picture this whole retelling in your mind and how, in a single moment, God backed his friend, David? God gave David the greatest victory he could have ever imagined or aspired for. This is indeed a much bigger deal than killing a bear or fighting with a lion as the Bible tells us when David often had to fight to protect the sheep. You can see the love of God being displayed the moment David ran toward the giant and cast the stone.

The question left to answer is, where did David find such strength and confidence, valiancy and authority? Well, it is very simple as it all came down to his strong relationship with HIS dear and great friend, the God of Israel.

When we, the church, spend time with the Father, we obtain a supernatural strength which can't be found anywhere else other than the secret place. Strong Christians make strong warriors and intimate friends of God. We can look at many examples of great strength in the Bible such as Samson, Gideon, and many other generals who marched through this planet, living out their faith based on a really amazing and particular relationship with God. As the Word says,

"God is our refuge and strength, an ever present help in trouble." (Psalm 46:1)

Strength is equivalent to confidence and confidence only comes from knowing HIM and knowing the power of His Word. David knew Him and therefore he was able to walk with confidence and confront the giant. Many Christians are not very confident and when the enemy comes and rocks their boat, many begin to wonder if they are going to perish. One example of great strength is Paul's difficult and challenging trip to Rome. When the ship he was on suffered a great tempest and was finally shipwrecked, no one came to their rescue. What we can learn from this great Apostle of faith is that despite the circumstances, he never lost "confidence" and his strength levels were always on the rise. Paul had to be a go-getter and his character had to be strong, as no one could have survived what he went through without giving up or denying his faith. What really touches my heart is the supernatural intervention of God's power invading Paul's reality, when in a time of desperation, an angel came and encouraged the Apostle and gave him strength. This account of the supernatural reminds me of another story when Jesus was fasting for forty days and nights. The Bible says that angels came and sustained Him and even ministered to Him.

God wants to invade our reality with His presence everyday and bring the extraordinary into our mundane day-to-day life. The perfect place where one can find strength, power, and vitality is in the presence of the Great I AM. Often when I have felt tired and weary after long days of ministry and powerful events, I go before His presence to get my shot of energy for the day. I am telling you folks, spending time with God will give you more energy and strength than any red bull or energy drink you have ever taken in your life. Your spirit was created to spend time with its Creator and the only way your spirit can be strong is by having a healthy and balanced diet and that can only be found in the presence of God.

Spiritual warfare can be very draining and can often lead to unexpected situations. The enemy is not waiting, pleasantly sitting and looking at how much you are overcoming. There is a point where he tries to engage you in some sort of warfare and bring opposition to bring God's plans down and defeat you in combat. God's friends are His best soldiers in His army, as they know how to hear from Him, wait on Him, and obey His voice. One must have a strong relationship with the best Sergeant of all in order to take illogical steps of faith, to win logical battles. The problem with many believers is that they put their logic before their faith and that's when the enemy takes advantage. Sometimes we need to take challenges of faith in battle without asking why and how. That's the most crucial point in our relationship with God, learning to let go and hold on to the invisible yet invincible One! We may not see Him with our naked eyes in the natural but we can sure see Him in the spiritual realm going before us and fighting with us!

As a boy preacher going from place to place, I soon realized how real the supernatural was and the reality of the enemy's workers and allies. Yes, I am talking about witch doctors and Satan worshipers who are not part of a fairy tale or somewhere in one's imagination. They work ferociously to deceive the world and to help the devil with his agenda. That reality of often meeting a witch doctor in the streets or having an encounter with an evil force, who was trying to upset me, was the reality on many occasions while doing ministry in highly spiritual dark places. Often it felt like my dad and I were walking into the enemy's land mines. One time, when I was preaching in India and staying at the 11th floor of a beautiful hotel in the heart of the city of Chennai, a demon came while I was asleep and made such a strong noise as if someone had thrown a stone against the window of my hotel room. It was 3:00 in the morning and I was suddenly awakened by the horrible noise. When I got up, I felt a very dark presence in the room. Immediately, I started praying in tongues and rebuking the evil forces and commanded them to back off and leave me alone. After 30 minutes of non-stop prayer and intense warfare, the atmosphere in the room changed as His presence filled the room. After that I proceeded to open the curtain and I saw that there were no trees or any trace of objects that had fallen onto my room's balcony. I was more convinced that the enemy was not very happy because of the youth meeting that was going to happen the next day, where more than 6000 youth came together and many of them were set free!

We all know the enemy is defeated and that Jesus our Lord and Savior has given us triumph over the kingdom of darkness. Nevertheless, we cannot be oblivious to the ongoing threats of the enemy and the constant battle that we all deal with one way or another in our lives. You know that two of the greatest lies of the enemy are: (1) that he doesn't exist and that anything that goes wrong in your life or any apparent spiritual or even physical attack is the product of mere coincidence or the fruit of an accident, and (2) that God has forsaken us when we go through trials and tribulations. On many occasions believers will hear these lies whispered in their ears. However, living in denial and not using the authority God has given us is surrendering to the enemy's tactics and giving up on His plans for our lives. I am not implying that the devil is involved in every day or hour of your life and that you must be casting him out 24/7, however, it is a reality that we must face him, not in our strength but with God's alone! We must be competent soldiers knowing that He will come back one day and reward our faith and acts of bravery! God wants to raise a generation of warriors, who are worshipers in the spirit, and who have a solid friendship and strong ties with the anointed one – Jesus the victorious one!

Chapter 6

Stewards of His Glory

Many of God's friends have always made the difference in their nations and territories, and the hand of God has been with them in all the various stages of their journey. As we know, every seventy years there is an emerging of a new generation. This present generation seems to be the one that God is raising in the midst of scarcity of vision and a multitude of sins. The Bible says,

"Where sin increased, grace increased all the more." (Romans 5:20)

This is a generation full of God's grace which will prophetically announce the revealing of his apostolic troops, prophets and pastors.

This can be likened to when God raised up Samuel and installed him in Eli's place, or when God raised up David and established him instead of King Saul. There was no one else in Israel that God could talk to except young Samuel. This child was marked since he was in his mother's womb. As Samuel grew up in the temple and devoted his life to God's service, he grew in intimacy and favor with God. As he transitioned from a boy to a young man, he matured and expanded day by day in his knowledge of the presence of God. Now imagine for a second how horrified and disgusted Samuel must have felt when he heard, in the middle of the night, how Eli's sons brought young women into the temple and slept with them. As the Scriptures record, God was very disappointed with Eli's poor leadership and for allowing his family relationships to be more important than his relationship with God! God rejected Eli and chose Samuel over him to be the new priest and judge for God's people over Israel. Samuel was entrusted with great responsibilities as a priest, judge and prophet over the nation. God doesn't trust these great tasks to anyone but to the one who is willing to live in His presence! That's the key to build a strong liaison with Him – trust is equivalent to time.

God is announcing the ushering in of a new priesthood to the world. Where are the Elishas who can take up the place and mantle of prophet, and where are the youths like David who can take the kingdom and reign? Where are the Samuels who can receive the revelation and are the priesthood of the new covenant? Where are the vessels that are willing to be molded? Where is the generation that is disposed to pay the price of the alabaster perfume to pour out upon Jesus' feet? God is seeking for vessels of honor which he may trust with His glory. Good qualifications don't gain friendship with God. The beautiful intimacy of God trusting in you and Him depositing His glory in you is the result of friendship that has been created on the basis of companionship. In this way, if God has confidence in you, He will deposit His glory and the perfume of His anointing into your vessel, and if you are a good administrator of His glory, He will continue increasing His trust in you. This also means that God will trust in you, in the same measure that you seek Him and are faithful to His friendship. The Bible affirms that to him who is given much, much will be expected (Luke12:48), which is the key to being a good steward of His glory.

Remember that occasion when the disciples of Jesus were trying to cast a demon out of a boy. The boy's father came to Jesus very flustered and expressed his frustration after seeing that the disciples weren't able to set his child free. After that, Jesus walked into the crowd and commanded the demon to leave the boy. The boy was set free and healed from that moment. The disciples, with mixed feelings of puzzlement and bewilderment, walked back with the Master. One of them dared to break the silence and ask, "Master, why couldn't we cast out the demon?" He then turns around and with a firm yet gentle voice replies, "This demon can't be cast out except by prayer and fasting." That's IT, that's the key to being trusted with the supernatural! God wants to entrust you with His glory but He first wants to get to know you. Prayer and fasting is the best way to lay down our flesh and live in oneness with Him. Intimacy is one of the best ways to gain trust with your spouse. Intimacy fosters a good and healthy ground for marriage and thus produces a special trust between a couple as they get to know each other deeply in the marriage journey! It is the same with God, the more time we spend with Him the stronger the bond we have with Him. God desires for a generation of men and women who He can entrust with the richness of His glory! Would you want to be one?

Chapter 7

The Greatest Lie!
The Greatest Truth!

The greatest lie separated us for a while

After everything had been created, God assessed His creation and saw that everything was good. He then decided to create someone whom would be a perfect image of Him on planet earth. He created Adam and put him as an administrator over all created things in paradise. God even gave Adam such wisdom that he was able to name everything from plants to animals and colors to numbers. God also decided to create someone special who would help Adam look after the garden, and that's when He created Eve out of Adam's rib. Both of them were really happy and had been granted the blessing from God to look after every precious thing He had made. God gave them permission to eat of every single plant and fruit tree. Nonetheless, they were warned not to eat of the tree of the knowledge of good and evil. One day, while Eve was cultivating flowers and taking care of the garden, a wicked serpent came out of nowhere and spoke to Eve. As we all know, this serpent was the Devil who took serpent form in order to tempt Eve. When Eve looked at such a strange crawling creature, she asked herself why perhaps this malicious animal was alluring her to eat the forbidden fruit. Nevertheless, she restlessly couldn't bear such temptation and gave in to the serpent's offer. After a while, pondering what God had said about that tree and what, on the other hand, this evil snake was telling her, she decided to give it a try. When she did eat it, immediately she ran to look for Adam and invite him to try the forbidden fruit. When Adam looked shocked at what Eve had done, and without remedy, he himself gave in and ate a piece of it as well. Meanwhile in heaven, God was concerned with Adam and Eve's welfare so He decided to come down and check on them. When He came down, He realized both of them were hiding and covering themselves and after a little while, God called Adam, "Adam, where have you been?" He asked. A few seconds passed by and Adam and Eve came out of the bush and told God everything that had occurred. (This is my paraphrase of Genesis 2 and 3.)

That same day God's heart was broken, and unavoidably, He had to take them out of the Garden of Eden. His first creation had betrayed him due to Lucifer's lie and malevolent plan to overcome God's creation. Just imagine for a second what God must have felt in that instant when Adam and Eve listened to the serpent and were deceived by the plot Satan cunningly planned against God's creation. This evil lie didn't remain in the garden and die there but had ramifications for generations to come.

For generations, many of God's friends embraced the lie and fell into the trap of Satan. One real example was Cain, who disobeyed God and killed his brother, Abel, becoming the first murderer in human history. Another one was Esau, who transgressed his friendship with God when he sold his birthright for a plate of lentils, and Eli, who allowed sin to enter the priesthood by his sons, and for this reason his friendship with God was wounded. We can also name King Saul, who broke off his friendship with God by trusting in his own strength and consulting a medium. The list goes on and on for thousands of years!

There exists a great truth here to recapitulate: God created the Garden of Eden to dwell in with man, but when man sinned, God's heart was saddened greatly that He had to make the hardest decision, to separate His glory from the most beautiful of all He had created – Humankind. For this reason, the Bible declares,

"All have sinned and fallen short of the glory of God." (Romans 3:23)

As this became the cruel reality in this world, darkness permeated the earth and Satan and his fallen angels corrupted all humanity. Except for Noah, one of God's genuine friends, who despite his unpopularity as he was not like other men, won God's trust. He was given the task of building one of the biggest engineering projects ever done up to that time in history. He was to build the biggest ship which was going to serve in God's redemptive plan to protect Noah, his family and every kind of animal and specie from the darkest fate; a great flood that would wipe out the rest of the human race, unlike anything ever witnessed or seen on planet earth to that date. God's redeeming plan succeeded and after forty days of Noah sailing in the ocean, he and his family arrived to a new land which they were going to call home. The greatest lie couldn't stop the Father from pursuing His greatest dream!

The greatest master plan to redeem humanity again and restore the broken relationship with creation was being drafted and written in the pages of history. If we look deeply into the Scriptures, we can see how God preserved the seed of righteousness to bring a Savior and a Redeemer, who later we see was His own Son, who gave Himself up to restore the broken bridge. Jesus Christ and God's plan for redemption was thought and spoken about even from the moment the first lamb offering was offered and accepted for the forgiveness of the sins of Adam and Eve and the generations to come. For many generations, lambs and goats were offered as an offering of redemption until the day the Lamb of God, Jesus Christ, paid the price for our ransom and gave Himself as a living offering to restore the path for friendship between the Creator and His creation. God was and always will be passionate about bringing His children back to the garden of His presence!

The greatest truth restored us all

The foresaid separation lasted a short time however, because the Creator's desire to dwell with His creation is so mysterious and profound that He Himself made animal skin garments for the first human beings. The question that could arise here is, "How did he make them?" The Bible does not offer us further details, but from the beginning, He chose the lamb to be a symbol of atonement for the sins of human beings. The words "skin garments" indicates to me that God may have sacrificed a lamb to sew clothes for His children, Adam and Eve. If this is so, and this was the first of many lamb sacrifices during more than 4000 years, then evidently it becomes clear that the sacrifice of a perfect lamb offered for the great cause of restoring God's friendship with His creation, remains the pattern God requires.

This is how I imagine it could have been: There would have been a great silence in heaven when the Father exclaimed, "Who will go? Who will go for us? Who will save them? Who will be the eternal sacrifice?" Suddenly He heard the voice of His Son proclaim, "I will go Father and do your will!" The Father's heart rejoiced and a huge smile was painted across His face when Jesus finished saying these words. The angels lifted their voices in praise of the Lamb of God, and the twenty-four elders prostrated themselves and threw their crowns at His feet and adored Him. There would have been a great celebration; it was a day of rejoicing because the enemy had come to his end.

It is for this cause that Christ, as the Lamb of God, offered himself and died on the cross, pouring out all His blood for love's sake and in compassion for us all. Dear friend, what great love is God's, who even offered His only Son and gave Him up into the hands of roman soldiers to be flogged, hurt, beaten and crucified, for one cause alone: TO RESTORE THE FRIENDSHIP OF THE FATHER WITH HIS CREATION.

> "For God so loved the world that He gave His only begotten Son, that whoever believes in Him should not perish but have everlasting life." (John 3:16)

Chapter 8

Celestial Encounters

The great patriarchs of the Old Testament had heavenly encounters which had great impact on their life and future. When Abram had an encounter with God, as it is told in Genesis 12, he understood the calling to leave his land and so proceeded to obey and please God. Abraham had encounters with God to the extent that God himself descended and spoke with him outside his tent. In one of these marvelous instances, God says to the patriarch, "count the stars," and he responds by saying, "Lord they are too innumerable to count." God then smiled and said, "So will your descendants be."

The Bible reports that many times God descended to speak with Abraham, and in Genesis 18, the Bible relates to us how the three angels descended in human form to announce the anointed birth of his promised son Isaac. God became Abraham's best friend so much so that he revealed his concealed secrets as well as His whole plan and purpose to him. In Genesis 18, we see in verses 23-33 how Abraham intercedes during an encounter with God, asking him not to destroy the city of Sodom and Gomorrah if only ten righteous men could be found. Lamentably, there were not even ten moral men and the judgment had already been decided. In verse 33, we see the profound intimacy God had with Abraham. In these encounters he spoke for many hours with Him and it was during these divine appointments that Abraham's destiny was marked and planned out. Every time that God spoke, Abraham obeyed because he knew God's sweet and authoritative voice, as did Moses during his encounter with God. Each encounter has a purpose and a mission.

Chapter 9

God's Confidents

Intimacy with God will enable us to hear with more clarity and perfection the voice of our Beloved. Our spiritual hearing will be more acute and therefore we won't have the dilemma, "Was that God speaking to me just now?" The ability of hearing His voice will become something very familiar even in our mundane day-to-day life. Intimacy with God will strengthen our hearing and therefore will sharpen our discernment in knowing how to distinguish when God speaks. There will be an indisputable and undeniable peace which will envelope us when we hear His sweet and yet powerful voice. Many believers don't know how to hear God so they depend on others to hear for them. Many justify their lack on intentional pursuit of hearing God by relying on others. One has to be very intentional when it comes to hearing from Him. When many folks pray, they don't spare a quiet time to sit in God's presence and wait for Him to speak. Rather they speak out, voice out, vent out, and ask for what their hearts want in the NOW! Many live happily and satisfied with hearing God from others. Please don't misunderstand what I am trying to say here and please hear me out. There is a much better dimension and much more enjoyable place to be with the Lord and that is to hear His voice on a personal and intimate level. Many of you are perhaps wondering and asking yourself, "How can I reach such a level in my life?" The answer can be very simple, but before I give you the answer, let me challenge your thinking today.

Have you reached a plateau in your spiritual life where you are depending on what others say from the Lord? Are you constantly searching for a prophet to get your prophetic doses for the day? Are you likely to always be in meetings waiting to hear some kind of directional word? I am not saying that you are not to attend a prophetic meeting or welcome a prophet into your house. On the contrary, what I am trying to say is that the tendency of relying on others can hinder your growth and therefore your prophetic development and ability to hear from God directly. God wants to speak to us openly and he would really enjoy it if we spent more time with Him so that he can teach us His ways. We would save ourselves so many heartaches and problems if we lingered in His presence and waited until He spoke to us. Nonetheless, as you grow spiritually and develop your prophetic sense of hearing, it is going to be a trial and error kind of journey. Sometimes you will miss God and sometimes you will get the message with perfect clarity and with no interferences. That said, we are not to be afraid of missing God because we are all learning, and as children have to hit the floor numerous times until they learn to master the art of walking, we also, as the body of Christ, must learn with an open heart and a humble spirit to hear God!

There was one time when I was invited to be the speaker at a rather large crusade in Pasto, Colombia. Pasto is a small border city in between Ecuador and Colombia. The hosting pastors had organized everything and the crusade had been long advertised. Back then I was living in Miami and I was very excited about returning to Colombia. During my prayer devotional in the days leading up to the crusade I heard the Lord saying, "Alejandro you are not going to Colombia." When I heard this voice it really shook me! I decided to put this thought in the back of my mind and I made out that it was the enemy trying to stop me from going to such a big rally! It just didn't make sense to me at the time that my Father would deter me from going to a city-wide crusade where many souls were going to be saved. Years later, I learned that we are not indispensable and that God will carry on with His agenda whether we are there or not. Frightened by the thought of canceling such an important event, I ignored the voice and went ahead with my travel plans. What I didn't know was that God was trying to protect me from something. Later on, I learned the guerrilla (a para militant organization), a day after the crusade was finished, had raided the city where I was supposed to preach. A number of incidents made my flight to Bogota a nightmare that day. The flight out of Miami was delayed and thus made me late for my connecting flight to Pasto. Mind you, that was the only flight out that afternoon before the time when I was supposed to preach, so it was cutting it really fine. When I got to Customs and was ready to clear immigration, there was such a long line of people that by the time I reached the immigration officer, it was too late and the possibilities of making the other flight were very unlikely as the hours passed by. It didn't matter what I did that day – everything was turning out wrong! After hurrying to get my bags and walking over to the domestic terminal to check-in for the other flight and also clearing security, they were already boarding my flight. To add to my disappointment and frustration of the day, when I got to the gate, it was closed. I watched as the plane was pulling off the runway. I felt like crying or even screaming out of sheer discouragement. However, after gathering my thoughts together, I decided to check into a hotel nearby the airport and wait for another flight scheduled for the following day. When I called the pastor and told him what had happened, he was very upset and flustered just like I expected. He had put so much effort into organizing the crusade and everybody was expecting the "Boy Preacher." I wasn't the boy anymore as I was in my teen years, and quite honestly, probably stubborn in my way of thinking. God taught me a big lesson through that experience! God has a very good sense of humor, as He will let you reach a certain point and then bring you back with love. Well that is exactly what happened to me. The next day I boarded the last flight out of Bogota as all of the other flights had been canceled due to bad weather. This was the plane I was supposed to be on the day before. When I finally made it to the plane, I sighed a sigh of relief. I thought after the whole adventure in Bogota, God was finally giving me the green light, but to make matters worse, when we were descending and as I was looking out the window at the beautiful high mountains that divide both countries, I heard the voice of the pilot through the intercom system saying, "Ladies and gentleman, due to bad weather, the runway has been closed and we are going to have to return to the nearest city and refuel so we can go back to Bogota as we are not allowed to land in this runway at nighttime." When I heard the pilot's announcement, I shed a few tears and if you could see my face, I was not a happy camper. My face reflected what was in my heart at that moment – disillusion, confusion and bemusement. I could not believe I had gone all that way and that God would only let me see the mountains and then send me back home. That was one of those BIG lessons your Daddy teaches you and after that you learn so much that you never dare or even contemplate the possibility of disregarding His voice.

God is calling a generation that leaves everything else aside and chases His presence; a generation that lives and breathes in God's presence; a church that encounters His glory every day and a people who is willing to say as psalmist David said,

> "Better is one day in your courts than one thousand elsewhere." (Psalm 84:10)

Chapter 10

A Passionate Generation

Passion is the thermometer that impacts your destiny and your present; it will cause you to do what you do with excellence. For example, if you are passionate about football, you will talk about football; you will know all there is to know about it; you will know all the players names and who are the best scorers. If you are passionate about computers, you will know which software is the latest, which programs are the most advanced, and you will also have some sort of knowledge about computer parts; or if you are passionate about acting, you will study your lines, become familiar with many plays and pour much time and hard work into rehearsals. The reality is that passion is the driving force that makes you do what you do with excitement, gladness, satisfaction, and perseverance. Hence, if you are passionate for Jesus and if Jesus becomes your best friend, you will know all about His majestic personality, and therefore you will also know the keys to opening the treasures that God has prepared for you. Remember that the keys are found at the feet of the Master.

You will know Him; you will see Him manifested in your

life and in your family; you will know what is pleasing to Him and so you will dedicate your life to the pursuit of His presence and will avoid grieving the Holy Spirit, by whom you were sealed.

> "...Having believed, you were marked in him with a seal, the promised Holy Spirit." (Ephesians 1:13)

I very much like Jesus' parables. In them is a glorious revelation about the kingdom of heaven. Matthew 13:44-46 teaches us that the kingdom of heaven is like a hidden treasure of great value. In the same way, friendship with the Holy Spirit is worth a valuable price, and so we need to always cultivate that relationship with the One who has breathed life in us. By doing this, He will entrust you little by little and will give you His precious treasures that are in store for you. The only way to open those treasures is by getting to know His heart and spending time with Him, and as you seek His face He will confide in you more and more until you reach a new level. Sadly, many say that they know God but are far from Him. Nevertheless, now is the time to take the treasure which God has given you by taking hold of the land God has given you to conquer. It is the hour to decide – friendship with God or friendship with the world? As Paul stated,

> "Whoever therefore wants to be a friend of the world makes himself an enemy of God." (James 4:4)

In John 17:15, Jesus prayed for His disciples and cried out to the Father saying,

"My prayer is not that you take them out of the world but that you would protect them from the evil one."

This prayer has impacted generations. In verse 16, which says,

"They are not of the world, even as I am not of it,"

He reaffirms that our kingdom is not of this world but is reserved in the heavens for those who persevere until the end. Passion will mark the difference in your work life, your marriage, your relationship, your profession and your business. More than anything, it will impact your prayer life because God has not called you to religion or religious traditions, but rather He has called you to a personal relationship with the Holy Spirit, your best friend.

The hour has come where your meetings become His meetings; this is the kairos moment of God over the earth. In these dangerous times mentioned in 2 Timothy 3:1, it is necessary to have a passionate heart for Jesus and for His Word, so that we may become part of the relentless generation Paul speaks of in Romans 8:35-38.

In one of his great tribulations, the Apostle Paul cries out with all his heart,

"For I am convinced that neither death nor life, neither angels nor demons, neither the present nor the future, nor any other powers, neither height nor depth, nor anything else in all creation, will be able to separate us from the love of God that is in Christ Jesus our Lord." (Romans 8:38-39)

The Apostle's passion is striking and it was because of this passion that he preferred to go to Jerusalem, to be bound and given over to the Roman soldiers to be imprisoned for the Gospel. I imagine this same man would have prayed entire nights for the great city of Rome, and for the Roman Empire.

One of Paul's dreams was to bring the powerful gospel of Christ to Italy and Spain. He spent years in prisons and courts, however Paul's faith did not grow dim, and even when he had been sailing for days without eating anything and was shipwrecked for weeks, he never lost passion for his mission. He even preached in the boat with the same encouragement he spoke with in Jerusalem and Ephesus. We find the associated verse in Acts 27:21 where Paul encourages the crew to fear not and trust in God. He stood up and said,

> "Keep up your courage...Last night an angel of God whom I serve stood beside me..." (Acts 27:22-23)

Romans 1:8 says,

> "First, I thank my God through Jesus Christ for you all, that your faith is spoken of throughout the whole world."

This verse reflects the passion that Paul had to preach the gospel. It is for this reason that Paul is called the founder of the Christian church in Rome and that passion is the same reason why today we have the gospel in our hands, because from Italy the word went into Europe and from England to the whole world!

Chapter 11

God's Generals

Dozens of men have marked the history of past generations, who God used in great revivals and history making events that have taken place around the world. Their faith and remarkable testimonies couldn't be summarized in one book. However, one such example is the evangelist Charles Finney, who was one of the men of his time who mostly preached travelling by horseback. History tells us that he rode hundreds of kilometers, bringing the gospel of Christ to all of England. His deep faith and driving passion compelled him to take the gospel into many townships. At times, he would walk into a bar where there were a few men drinking and partying and he would actually start preaching to them. The power of the Holy Spirit would hit the place and right there and then on the spot they would surrender their lives to JESUS. One of his faith stories was that he was at a train station and some of his old friends recognized him as he made his way into the station. However, when Charles saw them he felt the compulsive desire to preach his heart out to them. The moment he opened his mouth, preached the gospel and invited them to repent, they were struck down by the power of the Holy Spirit and convicted of their sins, surrendering their lives to Jesus at that very moment! Countless testimonies tell us of how wonderful and supernatural Charles's walk with Christ was. Perhaps some of you think, well, that was Charles and personally I don't think God has given me that measure of anointing. Dear friends, it wasn't his charisma that made many people convicted of their sins and ending up giving their lives to Christ; it was definitely beyond his personality. It was the power of the Holy Spirit that made it possible.

One time, Charles was standing underneath a tree and was deeply moved by the Holy Spirit. As he was standing there, he had a vision where he saw Jesus walking around the tree. As soon as he saw Jesus, he knelt down and worshiped Him and as he worshiped Him, Jesus revealed to him his calling. He took Charles's hand and invited him to walk and as they walked together, to Charles's amazement, Jesus was headed to a pub. Charles thought Jesus wasn't sure where He was going and so he stopped Him and asked the Lord why He was going to a pub. With a big and sweet smile, Jesus replied to him and told him, "Charles, that's where they need me most." Charles was stunned, but without hesitation, he walked into the bar and felt prompted to preach the gospel. As soon as he walked in, the men who were drinking and playing around were touched by the convicting power of Jesus and all of them (even the bartender) repented and surrendered their lives to Jesus. Wow, what an incredible journey it must have been for Charles to walk so close with the Lord!

At the end of the day, it is all about walking with God to witness His power manifested in our lives. If you want to see Him glorified in your life as Charles did, all you have to do is hold onto His hand and walk with Him. As you start a beautiful and powerful journey walking beside Jesus, you will realize that life is much easier when you live surrendered every day before HIS magnificent presence.

This is the time where you can impact your generation, family and community as you are being used by God to bring about a great revival in your city and nation! Remembering that these days are when we will live in one of the greatest revivals on planet earth, as the prophet Joel said,

> "...And afterward, I will pour out my Spirit on all people. Your sons and daughters will prophesy, your old men will dream dreams, your young men will see visions. Even on my servants, both men and women, I will pour out My Spirit in those days." (Joel 2:28-29)

And also, Haggai 2:7 says that,

> "the desired of the nations will come, and I will fill this house with glory."

As the cup of wickedness is being poured out over the nations of the earth, so we are also seeing the cup of fresh wine being poured out by God over the four corners of this globe. The hour has come where God is changing the guard and when He will give his inheritance to a new and fresh offspring – the Bride of Christ – the chosen ones! This church will raise the glory standard in the nations of the earth. Everything that past generations could not reach, we as a prophetic army will obtain. We will take this gospel to the ends of the earth! This is the time for you to decide to change the direction of your life and be part of this alliance of the friends of the Holy Spirit.

Passion will drive you to seek the Lord even with more desire and hunger for the supernatural! There are many people in this world that are and have been passionate to reach their unique goal. We can name many folks from Bill Gates to the first man who walked on the moon. These men were ordinary men but with a very distinct zeal. Their passion made them stand out among other men and caused them to fulfill their dreams and goals. Passion will take you to unchartered territory where the impossible is made possible and where the extraordinary becomes the norm in your relationship with God.

Often, as a boy, I use to spend hours in the presence of God. I wasn't content with just going to church and I wasn't going to settle with just being a nominal believer. I wanted more, and yes, I was desperate for more! My relationship with God became stronger and stronger as the months went by. My parents couldn't quite understand what was happening to their middle child. There was one time when my father came into my room and grabbed me and helped get me up. I was absolutely sucked into His presence and all I wanted to do was to remain there and worship. However, by this time, a few hours had already gone past and my dad's state of worry began to increase. He was not a believer, and so for him, this behavior that I was showing was very unusual and very difficult to understand. When he managed to drag me out, as I was laying on the floor, all he wanted to do was to check my face color as he related my white-paled skin with some sort of vitamin deficiency. That day, as was customary, he had bought a few bottles of multi-vitamins. I was really annoyed when he interrupted my time with the Lord because all I ever wanted was to remain at the feet of Jesus. My passion as a child became so strong that time didn't matter and nothing else took priority in my life, not even my studies, as all I wanted was to learn more of Him! That passion was the foundation ground which rooted me in the gospel and helped me overcome many trials and hardships during my early beginnings in the ministry as a boy preacher.

Chapter 12

A Burning Generation for the Gospel of Truth

We are living one of the most glorious seasons on the face of the earth. This is the time when God is going to raise up a generation that has vision, even when it becomes scarce.

"The boy Samuel ministered before the Lord under Eli. In those days the word of the Lord was rare; there were not many visions. One night Eli, whose eyes were becoming so weak that he could barely see, was lying down in his usual place. The lamp of God had not yet gone out, and Samuel was lying down in the temple of the Lord where the ark of God was. Then the Lord called Samuel. Samuel answered, 'Here I am.'" (1 Samuel 3:1-4)

It had become dusk and the sun was set on the horizon of Shiloh; the moon now appeared, announcing the night. The gates of the temple had been shut and a long day of priestly duties had finished. The boy Samuel assured himself that everything was in order, while the priest Eli prepared for rest before the lamp of God went out and ceased giving its light. On the other side in that very same sanctuary of God, a party was starting for Eli's sons, who were profaning the temple with adultery in the middle of the night. Displeased by all this sin and his heart enraged, God spoke to young Samuel, a young prophet in the making, who diligently helped the priest in all of his temple duties. In his chamber, the boy heard a voice both sweet and strong. Then he arose and ran quickly until he reached the priest's quarters, asking him if he had called him. Eli answered, "I did not call; go back and lie down." (1 Samuel 3:5) Somewhat confused, Samuel went and lay down. As soon as he heard the same sweet strong voice, he ran again to his master's room and asked once more if he had called. The priest was baffled and didn't know how to respond to him because he had already lost his priestly vision by that time. Eli had stopped hearing the voice of God, but when Samuel interrupted his sleep for the third time he perceived that God was trying to call him. With his mind tired and body worn out, Eli remembered precious moments in the Most Holy Place where he heard God's voice clearly. Just the fact that he had lost this wonderful contact by permitting sin in God's house was devastating to him. The priest remembered how God spoke to him in the past and when he did he would respond, "Here I am, speak Lord, for your servant is listening," and so he proceeded to give the boy the same instructions, saying to him, "son if you hear the voice again calling your name, just respond this way, "Speak Lord, for your servant is listening." Being a little puzzled, the child returned to his room and lay down on his bed. Suddenly he heard the same voice, however this time he knew what to do; he knew the secret of listening to God's voice. Samuel prostrated himself and uttered those words, "Speak, for your servant is listening." The heart of God was filled with an immense joy because he had found a new friend with whom he could share all His plans. Let's remember what the Bible says, that the Lord does nothing without first revealing it to his servants the prophets. (Amos 3:7) A new Prophet had been found and a new Judge for the people of Israel. From that moment, Samuel had received the mantle of a prophet over his life. The first secret that God revealed to him was Eli's sons profanation of the temple. God's voice then fell still, giving the boy over to tiredness and leaving him sleep; his heart was saddened by the news. (This is my paraphrase of 1 Samuel 3)

Dear friends, these are the days in which the lamp is at the point of going out in the hearts of many Christians who walk in religion and in the form of Christianity which the Apostle Paul spoke of, "having a form of godliness but denying its power." (2 Timothy 3:5a) Many are becoming content with little and entertained with much, simply going through the motions of attending church meetings. Let's remember that being a disciple of Jesus is more than just being part of a church or connect group. It is more than just being a regular church attendee, but rather being God's intimate friend.

Unfortunately, in these days, there is a lack of good and fresh bread in many "heavenly bakeries." The Word is becoming scarce in many churches and the gospel has been watered down with the purpose of not offending anyone. There is so much political correctness and fear of being rejected by the majority. We live in an era where the post-modern church has become so tolerant that it has forgotten its first love and neglected to keep pouring oil in the lamps of many vessels. As we know, it was imperative to keep oil in those old fashioned lamps to keep the fire burning and thus keep the light on. Back in those days, there was no electricity and this was the latest technology available to humankind. For years and for many centuries, people had to carry lamps lit up to have light in their homes. The Bible talks about the importance of having oil in our lamps as a symbol of carrying the presence of the Holy Spirit. If we recall what Jesus taught us in Matthew 25:1 which says, "At that time the kingdom of heaven will be like ten virgins who took their lamps and went out to meet the bridegroom," we see the relevance of carrying His oil in our lives. In many Biblical accounts the oil was mentioned as an instrument of healing and even a source of prosperity.

Many don't realize that by not preaching the true gospel many are being deceived and are living a "lite" Christian gospel lifestyle.

This is the time when God's heart cries out desperately for a generation of men like Samuel who will hear His voice, see the vision and keep the oil burning before the lamp goes out. God has called us to be visionaries. Let's bear in mind that many times the Scriptures compare us to eagles because, just like eagles, we have the same vision capacity and the potential to soar into the heavenlies. In these times where the vision is scarce, we need eagles with prophetic eyes that see further than the situation of the post-modern church and the evangelical fashions that, little by little, have distracted many Christians into abandoning the principle essence and foundation of all Christian history: a true relationship with Jesus. Remember that in the days of the Apostles, the disciples of Jesus became known as Christians, a term taken from the word "Christ"; the principle meaning of which is "to be a follower of Jesus Christ." More than just being followers, they were called Christians because they spoke like Jesus and performed the same signs and miracles He did, so much so that it was said the Apostles appeared to have spent much time with Jesus.

> "When they saw the courage of Peter and John and realized that they were unschooled, ordinary men, they were astonished and they took note that these men had been with Jesus." (Acts 4:13)

How glorious would it be if the whole church returned to the primitive way as in the days of the Apostles, carrying the power of the Holy Ghost from house to house and keeping their lamps filled with oil so the fires of revival keep burning across the nations.

The Scripture says that heaven and earth will pass away, but His Word never will! (Matthew 24:35) This is the eternal promise and hope for us, that he will bring a great awakening over all the earth as prophesied by the prophet Habakkuk, and that the earth will be filled with the knowledge of the glory of the Lord, as the waters cover the sea. (Habakkuk 2:14)

In Haggai 2:7, the prophet Haggai prophesied that the desire of all nations would come and make them tremble when the last greatest wave of revival washes over planet earth. Beloved, we are now in one of the most glorious seasons on earth, "the season of sowing." The gospel is being sown throughout the world and we are already seeing the first fruits of the harvest.

As we wait for the greatest harvest in the last days, knowing that our Savior Jesus Christ is coming soon and that these are times of preparation for His glorious return, we must wash our robes with the redeeming blood of the Lamb every day and walk in the power of the Holy Spirit.

As I have been walking with the Lord over the years, I have learned the difference between the genuine and the fake. I have seen the legitimate power of God and the man-driven power trying to run the show. It's heartbreaking when you see the church losing its real power and replacing it for a system, program or men-driven ideas.

One time, I was attending a conference where there was a guest speaker preaching from the United States. He had come to tour around Costa Rica and visit different churches of the denomination we belonged to. The first time I heard this man preach I had a check in my spirit which seemed strange to me, as seemingly, he was the MAN OF GOD. Many people flocked to his meetings fascinated by his strange ways of doing ministry. When I saw later what he was doing, I panicked and for the next forty-five minutes of that service I was trying to avoid him at all cost. I thought there was something wrong with me but then, later on, I found out the man was paying large amounts of money to some people to say they had been healed when all he was doing was practicing some sort of karate on them. I had never seen such wildness in a meeting. When I saw how this 6-foot-tall man would lift people in the air and let them drop, I then realized that there was something very wrong in the atmosphere of those meetings. As a skinny twelve-year-old preacher that I was, I was running for my life! The irony of it all is that I was helping that morning as an usher and was supposed to be catching people.

When I saw this spectacle and how he was talking to people and pushing them, my spirit was deeply grieved and all I wanted to do was to run from that meeting. Never had I ever felt such an urgent feeling of leaving church and going home. Later on I learned that this man ended up divorcing his wife and getting busted for buying people with money. Now I know why my spirit was so disgusted with this meeting and why I was restless during the service. What an incredible and vast difference between His authentic glory and the fabrication of the flesh.

Chapter 13

A Faith-Driven Generation

Faith is the open door to the supernatural and the only way to access this heavenly gate is by knowing Him in faith! God seeks a generation with a determined, active and enduring faith to entrust them with the riches of His kingdom. It is time for you to take the inheritance that God has promised you. To achieve this however, you will need to be prepared to grow spiritually and have an aggressive faith to claim the victory that has already been given to you. If we want to be intimate friends of His Presence, it is necessary that we believe in accordance with the Scriptures that God is indeed almighty and that through Him we will do great exploits.

> "With God we will gain the victory, and he will trample down our enemies." (Psalm 60:12)

Romans 10:17 states that,

> "Faith comes from hearing the message, and the message is heard through the word of Christ."

In order to have a fortified faith at all times, it is important that we nourish our spirit with His Word. Remember that faith is like a muscle that needs to be exercised in order to be strong and avoid deteriorating. You need to constantly exercise your faith and be aware that "our struggle is not against flesh and blood, but against the rulers, against the authorities, against the powers of this dark world..." (Ephesians 6:12) Jesus says however,

> "I have told you these things, so that in me you may have peace. In this world you will have trouble. But take heart! I have overcome the world."
>
> (John 16:33)

He has given us the victory in all areas of our lives. All we need to do is claim it as part of our inheritance as children of God!

Faith heroes list

Daniel was found praying to God when the nation he lived in had approved the wicked edict King Darius could ever pass during his reign. Nevertheless, he took a determined stand of faith and stood by his conviction.

According to Daniel 6:6, the king was pressured into passing the edict by a group of evil men who were jealous of Daniel. This new law was also designed to affect all the men and women who worshiped and served the God of Israel. Daniel was a young man who found himself among those exiled from Jerusalem, one who had the habit of praying three times a day. His passion for God and fervent faith sustained him during those days when men were talking anxiously about the new law and the consequences for those who broke it. In faith, Daniel did not bow before the persecution that had risen up against the Israelites. His heart continued to trust in God and he never ceased praying, even during such a difficult time. One day, some of the king's satraps and wise men which had incited him, found Daniel praying and informed the authorities. Immediately, he was brought before King Darius who was pressured to carry out the penalty for disobeying the edict as had been established. The king sought a way to save Daniel's life, but without any success. With pain in his heart, he gave Daniel over into the soldiers' hands. I cannot tell you beloved reader if there were thoughts in Daniel that could have tempted him to go back on his word, but above all his trust in the God of Israel prevailed against any other outcome. It was a crucial moment – Daniel would be thrown into a den of hungry lions, having determined that there would be no other way his life would be saved except by God's hand.

This passage impresses me personally, to know that Daniel was not distressed and that even as they were lowering him into the den, his heart did not fail him. God had already sent angels to rescue Daniel! The Bible tells us the angels of God stopped the furious lions' mouths. The following morning, the despairing king went out from his bedroom to the den where Daniel had been thrown, and upon arriving, he learned that the true and faithful God had rescued Daniel.

Sometimes we find ourselves in moments when we are persecuted and threatened by different situations in life. Occasions when our faith is challenged and tested as gold is refined by fire. Those are times in which we need to meditate upon His Word. In such situations, that's when we have to speak His promises over our lives and make them ours. So when the enemy targets us, we would never bend ourselves for one instant before the evil one's offers and threats. Let's keep in mind that our God is the most victorious one and that He will always give us the victory at the end of the day. As the Scriptures say in Ephesians 4:8:

> "When he ascended on high, he led captives in his train and gave gifts to men."

He took captivity captive back on the cross of Calvary, and as a result of such a victorious battle, He was made triumphant over the kingdoms of this world. He defeated death and sickness and above all he made US, the church, victorious ones! He didn't just win the trophy but he actually passed it on to another generation. A generation whose faith was a valuable shield to continue the greatest work He started on this earth.

Remember friends that Christ has triumphed over death. He took all our sins and sicknesses on the cross of Calvary more than 2000 years ago and annulled every act of evil, making us free through His death and resurrection and by His stripes we have been healed (Isaiah 52:5).

When I meditate upon this Scripture, I take into account that this is an absolute truth that was established in the past and has been validated for all generations. I want you to know that in Christ we are not only healed today but rather we were healed. This implies that there is a past legal right Christ left for us signed with HIS own precious blood. As the Word says in 1 Peter 2:24:

> "He himself bore our sins in his body on the tree, so that we might die to sins and live for righteousness;

by his wounds you have been healed."

This means that the covenant has already been established and that more than two thousand years ago he took sickness captive. All we must do therefore is confess and believe in these truths that are valid for all eternity. An active faith is what is needed to shake the earth and even the heavens! Numerous times the Bible speaks to us of the prodigious stories of men and women who marked their generation with an unyielding faith that sustained them even in the most chaotic times! Daniel was one of them and today you can be one of them. God is inviting you to walk on an amazing faith journey and be part of this generation that will continue writing the pages of history! Will you do it?

I remember one opportunity when I was asked for the very first time to pray for someone with cancer. I was only 11 years old and I was preaching at an outdoor meeting in my hometown, "Alajuela Costa Rica." This was my second or third time preaching at the park during this rally. A missionary, who became my mentor in ministry, organized it and hosted it for nearly a year. This evangelistic adventure turned into a revival experience as many people began to congregate in the park to hear the boy preacher. I was not even finished with my primary education and God decided that it was my time and so He launched me into full-time ministry! During those meetings, this lady came to hear the message. At the end, a frail, sick looking, and very skinny lady approached me and asked me to pray for her. She looked like she was fading and all I could see was a spirit of death all over her. In my premature discernment as a young preacher, I didn't know what to make of it. When I laid my hands on her, all I felt was the fire of God being unleashed out of my hands. Next thing I knew when I opened my eyes is that she was lying on the ground. She had been hit by the power of the Holy Spirit! That morning she left and with a big smile said, "Thank you 'little pastor.'" For the next two weeks I kept asking myself what had happened to this lady. I hadn't seen her and it seemed all very strange to me. What I didn't know is that this lady was related to my dad's family and that she had been diagnosed with liver cancer. Two weeks later, the same lady that had come with a downcast face had a different look about her. I remember she was so happy and the first thing she did was come around and give me a big hug. With tears streaming down her face and trying to gather the words, she told the missionary and my parents what had transpired after we prayed for her. She had been healed of cancer, and as astonishingly as that sounds, she had the doctor's reports in her hands. All she could do was sob while trying to let us know what the Lord Jesus had done in her life. That day my faith was increased and that was like an appetizer for what the Lord was going to do in Venezuela during my first mission trip. Many healings and miracles were witnessed during these meetings. Hundreds of souls came to Jesus and many doors were opened. That trip was the springboard to launch me into full-time ministry during my boyhood.

Chapter 14

Growing in Faith

Ephesians 4:13 says,

"until we all reach unity in the faith and in the knowledge of the Son of God and become mature, attaining the whole measure of the fullness of Christ."

Faith is the principle ingredient needed to grow into the stature of a perfect man. Many Christians have misread their spiritual growth, determining their maturity by their position in the church, years of experience, or certificates they have obtained. Although these basic things may enrich our lives spiritually and academically, faith is the principle measurement to determine one's maturity. Maturity is not gauged by the years of experience one may have in Christianity, but rather by the character one has developed in the presence of God. It is most valuable for our spiritual enrichment and personal faith growth to spend time in the secret place. How can our faith be enlarged if we don't spend time with our Creator. It is imperative for this generation of believers to expand their faith by depending on the one and only true source and that is "Intimacy with our heavenly Father."

The generation of new wineskins God is raising up is aware of the necessity of putting into practice these three principles:

1. Reaching unity in the faith.
2. Growing in the knowledge of His presence.
3. Coming into the stature of the perfect man and thus attaining the fullness of Christ.

1. Reaching unity in the faith

God is not impressed by our eloquent prayers or works of charity, but only by our faith. There is nothing that can move the hand of God more readily than the faith of one willing to stand up and make a difference. Only by being determined and leaving the comfort zone can we conquer the inheritance Christ has left us. It isn't important what title you may have, your age, ethnicity, culture, background or where you come from. He has guaranteed us that if we trust in Him, He will perform great wonders through us and thus use us to continue His work by advancing His kingdom every single day.

God commanded Joshua to cross the Jordan River and even though it seemed an impossible assignment, he was faithful and obeyed God, seeking to seize the Promised Land. The same God who was with Moses backed the young man. We read that Joshua said to the people,

"Consecrate yourselves, for tomorrow the Lord will do amazing things among you." (Joshua 3:5)

The people were to purify themselves and get ready because on the following day they would witness something glorious. It was then that the Jordan's waters were divided and the people were able to pass through on dry land. This shows us that there is a moment when God moves His hand supernaturally in favor of His people. God could have allowed His people to go through the Jordan the previous day, but rather He wanted them to rest after their long journey and surprise them the next day. This event was so historic it brought fear to all Israel's enemies and let the known nations of the earth know there was a God more powerful than the ones they worshiped, one who was defending the Israelites at all cost! The people had to wait for the moment when God would come through and they would all be ready to cross the Jordan River with great success. Not only was there a manifestation of the supernatural but an increase of their faith. If we pay attention closely and read deeply into the Scriptures, we learn that they were asked to rest the day before and ready themselves for the great exploit. It is necessary and vital for His people to rest in His presence so that their faith is strengthened. The only way to grow in faith is by knowing Him on a daily basis. The recipe for success in our faith journey is spending time at His feet and gleaning off His wisdom and never-ending love. Devoting time with our Savior and delighting in His presence will sharpen our faith character! The Psalmist David said,

> "Delight yourself in the Lord and he will give you
> the desires of your heart." (Psalm 37:4)

As the Apostle Paul wrote, it is necessary to grow in faith

to come into a superior level of the knowledge of His presence. This means that faith is the first level, or in other words, the first stage. Just as it is important that we achieve good grades in elementary school in order to graduate to high school, and just as we may aspire later in life to graduate from university with a degree, we need to undergo a process in the body of Christ to reach maturity.

> "And the God of all grace, who called you to his eternal glory in Christ, after you have suffered a little while, will himself restore you and make you strong, firm and steadfast." (1 Peter 5:10)

If any area in your life or family is to change for the better and for greater things to occur in your daily walk with your friend Jesus, the primary need is to build up your faith in order to lay down a strong foundation. If your faith is not matured and you don't grow it as you are meant to, then what will happen as a consequence is that when the times of hardship come and storm the boat of your life, your faith may not be as strong to endure the fierce gales of doubt that may hit your mind. Faith can be compared to the big canvas sails on an old sailing ship needed to propel the ship. The canvas sails were essential to catch the winds and to keep the ship sailing smoothly. Without them the ship couldn't go anywhere, as it was the elemental instrument required in the old day nautical technology to sail the ships across the big oceans! Without faith it is impossible to navigate through life and all the challenges that life can bring along! Faith in our heavenly Father will sustain us even in the weakest points of our lives. Faith is a number one step for any Christian! Faith is the key ingredient to see God's supernatural reality in effect in our lives and families every day! God wants to invade our reality with His faith reality and that in itself will bring great and extraordinary miracles about!

2. Growing in the knowledge of the Son of God

As we grow in faith, we will also grow in our absolute dependence on His companionship and relationship. As we grow closer to God then our knowledge of Him will increase in our lives.

I became a parent about two years ago. After being married to my beautiful Australian wife "Rebekah" for two years, God decided to bless us with a beautiful baby girl and we named her "Carielle." Today she is almost two years old and as a toddler, I can sense that she is growing more and more to love spending time with me as a father. I am learning more about her than what I knew when I first saw her pretty wrinkly pink face with rosy cheeks. Carielle has been such a blessing to us and we truly enjoy spending time with her. At the beginning, when she first came into this world, it was all new to me. I enjoyed being a parent, but to be very candid, I wasn't as bonded with her as my wife was. Nevertheless, as I spend more time with her and get to know her, the more bonded I become towards her. Now all I have to do is stretch my arms wide open and she will come running to give me a hug. Now I am all the more enjoying my daddy dates with her and taking her for walks to the park as I can interact with her even more than when she first came into this world. The same way I have grown in my love towards her is the same manner you and I can grow in knowing HIM deeply and closely! All it takes is to set aside some time. It might take you days, weeks, or even months, but the more you persevere in your quest to pursuing God, the more real His presence is going to become in your life. My relationship with my daughter has grown and it's because of the time I have spent with her. It is the same as my relationship with my wife Rebekah or any other solid friendship that I have. Time is the key to build long lasting relationships! The more time you spend with God, the better the outcome is going to be!

When we determine not to just listen about Jesus and hear of His wonders but rather to seek Him deeply, that's how we can get to know Him more and more each day. In the midst of this intense pursuit, sometimes we can find ourselves swimming in an ocean filled with treasures. Because of the great depth of beauty surrounding us, it becomes necessary to dive deeper in order to better contemplate each wonderful facet of God's person. I use this analogy of navigating the deep sea because of the unfortunate reality that we are seeing across the body of Christ. Some say they know of the Lord but when you ask them, "When was the last time that you had an encounter with God? When was the last time His glory saturated your room or the last time that you were dazzled by His glory? When was the last time that you were visited by His presence?" a great majority respond sincerely, "It was some time ago," while very few would reply "a few hours ago." This is because of the popular belief that many Christians hold today, that because we exist in a society that is becoming busier and more demanding of our time each day, it is more difficult to dedicate time to reading the Word, praying, meditating and simply resting in Him. The enemy will try to make us buy into these lies so that we don't spend time with

God. In fact, he will go to any length to inhibit us from going anywhere close to the Holy Place. The evil one will try all of his old tricks to distract us and snatch our time away from being in the presence of the Almighty God! This doesn't take away the fact that God is in control and that we are more than conquerors. The moment we draw the line and put an attack plan in action, we will overcome these temptations and we will triumph over our flesh and the evil one. God has given us such authority to put the enemy in his place and we are reminded in the Scriptures in Psalms 91:13-14 (NKJV):

> "You shall tread upon the lion and the cobra, the young lion and the serpent you shall trample underfoot. Because he has set his love upon Me, therefore I will deliver him; I will set him on high, because he has known My name."

As you can see, this is the Father saying to the church, "I have given you authority to tread upon your enemies." If you focus on the words "known My name." You will see a great kingdom reality here. The kingdom of God is about knowing Him!

> The Hebrew word "know" (yada), which is a common root in the semitic languages, has a wide range of meanings depending upon the context in which the word is found. Like our word "know" in English, the Hebrew word can indicate mental knowledge, that is, that a person "understands" or "has knowledge" of something, as when we say "I know that 2 + 2 is 4." But the concept of "knowing" something or

someone takes on a special meaning in the semitic languages, and this specialized meaning has to do with relationship, and primarily a relationship that is based upon the making of a covenant. We know this not only from the Hebrew Bible (Old Testament or Tanach) but also from literature outside of the Bible from the Ancient Near East.[1]

As we grow in His knowledge and the knowing of His presence, we will be able to rest and let go because when we rest in His presence, it is a sign of trust. You can say, "God I trust you and I believe in you," but those words may not carry the same validity as when a person trusts in the Word and also lives by His Word. When we know Him, we trust HIM and subsequently He will trust us.

Let's be mindful that each day has its own problems;

"Therefore do not worry about tomorrow, for tomorrow will worry about itself. Each day has enough trouble of its own." (Matthew 6:34)

If each day then brings its own concerns, what we are to do is put everything in God's hands and not worry because ultimately He will care for us. It is also important to dedicate a special time with God every day, and by doing so, we are able to build a beautiful bridge of trust between the beloved Holy Spirit and us.

God wants to entrust you today

Many people have come to me and asked, "How can I

---

[1] (Hegg, T. (n.d.) The Hebrew Word (yada') As a Covenant Term in the Bible and the   Ancient Near East. Retrieved from: http://www.torahresource.com/EnglishArticles/Yada_as_Covenant_Term.pdf)

have communion with God?" My answer is very and simple and practical, "Set apart time for God!" Begin to build confidence in Him, seek his face above all and remember,

"...seek first his kingdom and his righteousness, and all these things will be given to you as well." (Matthew 6:33)

Dedicate a special time of your day to God. Now by this, I am not speaking about going to church or watching the Christian TV channel (which are both good things, incidentally) but rather, I am referring to devoting time alone with your heavenly Father. Just as Jesus instructed us,

"...when you pray, go into your room, close the door and pray...then your Father who sees what is done in secret, will reward you." (Matthew 6:6)

A solid and long lasting friendship with God can be likened to when you were getting to know your boyfriend or girlfriend, when you spend time with your husband or wife, or when you spend time with your children. Often God uses our earthly relationships to be a mirror of our heavenly relationship with Him.

The supernatural and unique bond that God the Father wants to have with us is seen in the close relationship He had with Jesus, His Son, during His short time of ministry on earth. Jesus always pointed to His Father and gave Him glory for the miracles He witnessed during His ministry. One reference that can expand this notion is found in John 5:19:

"Jesus gave them this answer: 'Very truly I tell you, the Son can do nothing by himself; he can do only what he sees his Father doing because whatever the Father does the Son also does.'"

This bond between God the Father and the Son is a prototype of the relationship we are to have with our heavenly Father. Another image that God uses is that of a husband and wife – to be a representation of Jesus and the Bride of Christ.

Now, continuing with this picture of a husband and wife, here is why it is so important for us to spend time alone with God. If you were seated on public transportation with your spouse in a crowded train compartment, your conversation with your spouse would most likely be very different from an intimate conversation you would have with them if it were just the two of you seated at a table having dinner in the privacy of your home. In the same way, if we try and squeeze our devotional time into our daily activities and routines, only putting in the bare minimum amount of time, we may not reach the depths of intimacy with God that He so desires to have with us. In other words, our communication becomes shallow. Rather, we need to prioritize correctly, placing our devotional times with God at the center of our day as a core around which we structure our daily activities. In this way, we will actually find that all else falls into place correctly. By strengthening ourselves in God first and foremost, we receive His wisdom and strength to accomplish all others tasks ahead of us rather than accomplishing less in our own fleshly strength. We will accomplish more by doing less if we understand the principle of being in God's presence before we even start our day.

Just like couples who have been married for many years sometimes revert to using communication sparsely and purely for conveying information, so our devotional times can become stale if we allow routine to come in between us and God. Our prayers can become one-dimensional, a line of communication simply to let God know our needs, rather than us sending out offerings of worship to Him to tell Him how much we love Him. Again, this can be likened to an earthly husband and wife relationship and those first head-over-heels-in-love days, when two human beings cannot get enough of telling each other that they love one another. In the same way, God wants our times with Him to stay fresh and exciting. So in summary, to create a bond of trust and love, it is necessary to dedicate time to getting to know the person you love. This is the same pattern in our divine relationship with the precious Lamb of God.

> "From everyone who has been given much, much
> will be demanded; and from the one who has been
> entrusted with much, much more will be asked."
> (Luke 12:48b)

When some people look at the successful track records of genuine and God-driven ministries, many wonder, "How did they get there?" What many don't realize is the sacrifices and the discipline taken to get there. God won't entrust His anointing to just anyone who is wasting time. One of the key kingdom resources that we must master is "time." When we become good managers of time, then we can easily make the transition and become good stewards of God's resources. One of many resources is the "anointing." The anointing is the essence of the presence of God. The anointing can be given by measures and not everybody carries the same anointing. Some people argue that we all are anointed and therefore we all carry the same anointing. God does love everyone the same way but that doesn't mean God will entrust everyone with the same anointing. The anointing is given to those who God can entrust with this precious treasure. By the same token, I am not being dogmatic in saying this is the only way God operates and is exclusive to only those who pray and fast. He is a sovereign God and He does what he pleases. I also know God is a gracious God and He can use an individual in a moment of faith and glory to move in the supernatural. However, that is not an indicator of how much anointing that person carries. A substantial and solid lifestyle in the supernatural can only be maintained by a constant pursuit of God and His presence, a daily surrender and a devoted and sold-out heart to Jesus!

There was one time in my life when God asked me to spend more time with HIM. He even challenged me and told if I spent time with Him, he would open the doors of the nations. As an 11-year-old boy, I didn't have a clue how to start and all I knew about spending time with God was fasting during school recess and praying at my favorite prayer spot which was a large stone placed on the school grounds. I began my prayer journey by giving up TV time after school and praying for one hour instead. This was rather hard but as days went by, my relationship with God became stronger and stronger. What I loved the most about those days was the supernatural manifestations during such prayer times. One hour became two, and two became three and so successively my prayer time became longer and longer. My hunger for the supernatural was not being quenched by a Sunday school service or by the church meetings. I wanted more of God and all that He had for me. Some of my fellow brothers and sisters in Christ who were part of my home church couldn't understand what God was doing in the life of this boy. Nonetheless, sometime later, I realized that God was preparing me for the ministry and that it was necessary for me to spend all of that time with HIM in order to manage what was about to happen in my life. Three years later, the same boy that went to Sunday school, did mimes and preached the gospel in connect groups around the small and rural town of "La pradera" was the same boy preaching to thousands in healing crusades in Colombia and other places in South and Central America. What God did in such a short amount of time could have become overwhelming for a teenager to handle. One of my greatest fears was becoming prideful or distracted. There was one thing that sustained me while I was at the peak of my ministry as the boy preacher and that was "my intimate time with God." Many questioned my longevity in ministry and even some said that it was going to be a transient time in my life and that as soon as I became a teenager, I was going to realize how difficult it was to keep up what I was doing. Many questioned my passion and my zeal for God and many questioned my parents harshly for not pushing me to be a normal child. Even the media on many occasions asked me, "If you could travel in time would you have rather spent time playing with your friends and being just a child than preaching the gospel?" My answer was a definite and resounding, "No, I would have never chosen or changed anything in my childhood."

Getting to know God will build a strong bridge in your relationship with the Holy Spirit and once you have stepped into that dimension, as the Word says, nothing will separate us from the love of God.

> "For I am convinced that neither death nor life, neither angels nor demons, neither the present nor the future, nor any other powers, neither height nor depth, nor anything else in all creation, will be able to separate us from the love of God that is in Christ Jesus our Lord." (Romans 8:38-39)

God wants to entrust you with His presence today, and so my friend, I want to encourage you to begin today by setting aside some time with your Creator. As you commence this journey, you will realize how much you will enjoy it and how much your spirit will want to remain in the secret place. Consequently, there will be a dying process where your priorities change and God becomes number one in your life. How can you say you know God if you don't spend time with HIM? Time spent with Him is the best investment in your life as it will affect your personal growth, character, family, and even your finances. God will honor those who honor HIM! (1 Samuel 2:30)

3. Coming into the stature of the perfect man and attaining the fullness of Christ

When speaking in these terms, Paul was referring to the process that all of God's people live constantly. It is the process of being alive in Christ and dying to the old man and the old nature.

> "You were taught, with regard to your former way of life, to put off your old self, which is being

corrupted by its deceitful desires; to be made new in the attitude of your minds; and to put on the new self, created to be like God in true righteousness and holiness." (Ephesians 4:22-24)

Paul speaks of a progressive and transforming process in which the human character becomes the character of Christ. Now, this is not an easy transition, but rather, requires death to many parts of our human nature in order to allow the Lord Jesus Christ to live and reign in our hearts. This is how the Lord transforms our mentality and the way we are, placing his personality in us. It is a season in which He molds us, when the Potter forms our vessels and conforms us to the perfect model, a model He designed to endure the different changes and transitions in life.

Many say that no one can be perfect while they live on this planet, and while that is true friends (as no one is perfect but God), in the meantime, we should strive for excellence and try to please God in every single area of our lives. Reaching the stature of the perfect man means that we grow into the character of Christ. The only way we can grow into His character is by knowing HIM! That's why it is so important to have time with God. The more we seek HIM, the more He is going to change us, as long as we allow Him to make those changes in our lives and in our minds. The essence of Paul's words to us is that if we change our mentality, we will change our way of living. There is a very important truth here, that as we think, so will we live. If we have a kingdom mentality, the result will be that we will live as royalty as the children of a mighty God. If you dedicate time to being in God's presence, He will begin changing your character, and then consequently, many areas in your life will be transformed, such as your mind, your vocabulary and even your life habits.

We must remember that it is not by our own strength that this transpires but by His Holy Spirit. Some people may think that these changes can be sacrificial and that therefore there is no grace. What we need to be mindful of is that when we spend time in His presence, these changes will occur day by day. There is no sacrifice given here because it is not us who are making those changes. Before you know it, you will realize that some areas in your life are shifting for the better. However, the secret to see this in action is the obedience and willingness to be changed in all areas of our lives. Many times we react from our human character in different situations and the results can be harmful, simply because we do not allow the Holy Spirit to act or we do not react with the character of Christ. When we don't die to the old man and we continue doing the same things, we will hinder God's process in our lives rather than advancing it. The factors of obedience and humility can accelerate God's changing process in our lives so that we can become more like Him!

Let's remember what happened to the people of Israel. Instead of crossing the desert in forty days, the process was multiplied – one year for each day, a total of forty years. Something that God had intended to take a few days was set back for years simply because the generation that had left Egypt did not understand God's patterns, His purposes and times. Throughout the journey, many gave themselves over to defeat because of fear and doubt. Only a handful of the first generation entered the Promised Land. It was the second generation, with their leader Joshua, who were able to enter and enjoy what God had promised the people of Israel as their inheritance. Due to their hardness of heart, idolatry, unbelief and lack of character, the majority of those who left the land of Egypt only heard, dreamt of and planned to enter the Promised Land. They never actually conquered what God had in store for them. Only those who understood God's purpose and followed him faithfully came to be part of the generation that partook of the fruits of the Promised Land.

It is indispensable to grow into the character of Christ so that our attitude can have a transforming influence on everything around us, so that we can truly set a different standard in the world, being as Christ said, "The light of the world." (Matthew 5:14) We cannot be the light of the world if we do not have enough oil in our lamps to keep them shining brightly. This is illustrated by the parable of the ten virgins who needed oil in their lamps while waiting for the coming of the bridegroom (Matthew 25:1-13).

One of the requirements in the Old Testament temple was that a fire be kept burning constantly. This was symbolic of God's presence continually dwelling with His people, and it demonstrates that we are to maintain constant communion with Him. Fire is also often mentioned in the Bible as a manifestation of the Holy Spirit (e.g. when the disciples were baptized in the Spirit for the first time in the book of Acts and tongues of fire appeared to rest upon their heads. Acts 2:1-2)

Communion with the Holy Spirit is also represented by oil; this is equivalent of the anointing. When a man was anointed king in ancient Israel and oil poured over his head, it was an act proclaiming God's favor and presence upon that man. This man was chosen by God and had fellowship with Him. Often they would bring this man, prophet, leader, ruler or king into a room and anoint him by pouring oil from an old goat horn. They didn't just put a little bit of oil on his forehead but rather wet him with oil. After such a public anointing ceremony, the anointed king or leader would go out and exercise his authority.

The parable of the virgins teaches us that we are to maintain fellowship with the Holy Spirit, faithfully keeping our lamps filled with His anointing and presence. By keeping the oil, we will keep our hearts burning until Jesus' return!

It is essential to be overflowing with His presence and make a difference in the world we live so that the light of Christ can shine in and through us. As the psalmist David said, "certainly my cup overflows." (Psalm 23:5) When the psalmist mentions these words, he is referring to nothing less than being overflowing with God's anointing.

The generation God is raising in these times is one of men and women with the character of Christ who are overflowing with joy, peace and a significant anointing. When they present themselves before the King of kings, their cups will not only be full but will overflow in a way that is contagious to their peers, work colleagues and family. They will affect the lives of the people around them not only with their words, but also with their acts. As the Apostle Paul said, may we be open letters read to the world (2 Corinthians 3:2).

I remember one time when we had finished an amazing, incredible and glorious meeting in Homestead, Florida, God was doing some remarkable things during these meetings. However, on the last evening of this revival, the presence of God was so intense that the meeting went on for almost four hours. Some of the manifestations were: miracles, prophetic words, angelic visions, and supernatural manifestations such as gold dust and oil in people hands. For those who may be reading this and haven't experienced this kind of supernatural reality, let me tell you my friend it is real! I have seen it over and over but mainly in meetings where His glory has saturated the atmosphere and it's not about the songs, the preaching or the program anymore but rather is about HIM! After finishing the meeting, the family that was hosting me took me home and while riding in the car with them, the glory was released again. They were crying and some praying while experiencing the joy of the Lord. The amazing thing is that when we reached home and knocked on the door, as soon as my friend's mother-in-law opened the door and we said hi to her, she was hit with the anointing and knocked by the power of God. There were some other ladies in the kitchen that night and the same thing happened to them. Before I knew it, we were experiencing a mini revival at the house where I was staying. The power of God can be so contagious!

> "Are we beginning to commend ourselves again? Or do we need, like some people, letters of recommendation to you or from you? You yourselves are our letter, written on our hearts, known and read by everybody. You show that you are a letter from Christ, the result of our ministry, written not with ink but with the Spirit of the living God, not on tablets of stone but on human hearts."
>
> (2 Corinthians 3:1-2)

We need to grow in the character of Christ to conquer the complete inheritance God has predestined for each one of us. Remember that we are co-heirs with Christ and by His grace he has made us "more than conquerors" (Romans 8:37).

Surrender to the Lord the areas you think need to be shaped in your life and I assure you that He will give you the victory in each one of them. The more time you invest in His presence, the closer you will come to the point of your encounter and transformation!

Chapter 15

Going After the Double Portion

God is preparing an army of men and women who will make radical decisions for Christ. We are radical for Him when we are not satisfied with the status quo, but rather we try to revolutionize the world and bring changes to our society by establishing the kingdom of God in our midst. We are radical when we are willing to continue moving forward, no matter what obstacles are presented before us along the way, like the prophet Elisha who continued until the end, even when he knew that God was going to take Elijah. In this way, he received a double portion of the spirit that had been upon Elijah when they came to the other side of the river Jordan:

> "Elijah took his cloak, rolled it up and struck the water with it. The water divided to the right and to the left, and the two of them crossed over on dry ground. When they had crossed, Elijah said to

Elisha, 'Tell me, what can I do for you before I am taken from you?' 'Let me inherit a double portion of your spirit,' Elisha replied." (2 Kings 2:8-9)

STOP

What spirit did Elisha speak of? If we see from a prophetic perspective, we understand that he spoke of the Spirit who dwelled in Elijah, the precious Ruach Hako'desh, or Holy Spirit.

We must be aware that in a society so thirsty for the supernatural reality, it is necessary that we be radical Christians, willing to bring changes in the midst of a society in need of perfect love – the love of Christ. To make radical decisions that benefit our society is not a choice that the enemy is going to like. The enemy is not threatened in the least by any Christian who usually attends church once a week and maintains a normal, comfortable standard of life. However, when the people of God understand His calling and purpose and begin to walk in line with fulfilling the goals that He has designed for them, the enemy certainly will not be happy. It is then that the opposition and battle begins for all those who want to make a difference in our culture.

To gain a deeper understanding of what happened to Elisha, we need to analyze what took place in 1 Kings 19 (*vv 19-21*) when Elisha was called. As we read this chapter, we see the supernatural way God suddenly impacted Elisha's life when all he was doing was simply plowing with oxen. This indicates that even though Elisha was going about his daily duties, he was at a place in his own heart where he was ready to move into all God had for him. There was also an obstacle that Elisha had to overcome at this point. Would he cling to the familiar comfort of his everyday life, of all he had known, or would he step out and respond to God's radical calling upon his life? I note that the first thing Elisha did when Elijah threw his mantle over him was to respond to the calling immediately. (He did not need to think twice before leaving the oxen and plough behind.) The second thing he did was say goodbye to his father and family.

Beloved reader, what was it that inspired Elisha to leave everything and follow a prophet, someone he had never met before and who was not known by his family? What was the key factor that caused Elisha to act hastily in this way? What touched Elisha in such a profound way that he abandoned everything and began to walk in a completely new direction? It was nothing other than the supernatural encounter he had with God and the transference of the Spirit of God onto Elisha, when Elijah's anointing-saturated mantle was thrown over him. He had this in his heart and mind. He was going after the mantle! And there was nothing that could stop such a determined man as Elisha. God wants to raise a people whose hearts are so determined to follow Him – a generation of believers that are not sidetracked by the distractions of this world and that are not about the business of this world but rather about the affairs of His kingdom, and whose pursuit is the triple portion. We now have the Holy Ghost in our midst and it is no longer a double but rather a triple blessing that will be bestowed upon every believer who believe firmly in God's supernatural plan!

Another factor Elisha had to overcome was fear. Why fear? Because if he was going to be a prophet of God, he would have to deal with the same intimidation and discouragement that Elijah had to deal with on numerous occasions. One such incident was when the sons of the prophets came to Elisha and told him that his master would be taken from him that day (1 Kings 2:5), implying perhaps that there was no point in him continuing on with Elijah as he was about to be taken up to heaven that day. Elisha was not daunted however and continued on his way with Elijah. The prophet's conviction to stay with Elijah and pursue his blessing was much stronger than any negative word. Elisha's response to the sons of the prophets is worded as a command; he literally ordered them to be quiet. Having done this, Elisha kept walking until he obtained what he had been astounded by in the past, dreaming of, and waiting for, for so many years – a double portion of His Spirit.

Beware of fire quenchers

This double portion would maintain his faith, his conviction and his dreams and goals, in spite of all that he had yet to go through. It should also be noted here that Elisha aggressively pursued more of God, more of His anointing and power upon his life, just as we must also do. We cannot expect to receive a powerful spiritual blessing from God without being committed to relentlessly seeking His face. All spiritual blessings are rooted in and grow out of cultivating a deep intimacy with God. Some people may be good-hearted and have good intentions by trying to help you manage your experiences with God. Sadly enough, there are so many fire fighters in church rather than fire keepers. Many people when they don't understand what God is doing tend to shut it down or control it. These prophets couldn't comprehend why Elisha was following Elijah so intentionally. We must be intentional when seeking God, because no matter what comes our way, we will be anchored to the roots of our faith and intimacy with Him, and that's what will keep us going in the times of turbulence and hardship in our lives. By no means am I implying that you shouldn't be accountable or share with other elders about your life or even your experiences with God. I think it is rather healthy for any believer to be in relationship with kindred-spirit folks, ones from whom you can obtain advice in the times when you may not know what is happening in your own spiritual journey. It is devastating when one who is so full of fire for God turns around and becomes confused in his own ways. When a person is no longer accountable or is not willing to accept others spiritual insight, then that person becomes a law unto himself. That's a very dangerous place to be! You must be able to discern if someone is trying to help you build your life or trying to discourage you by holding you back.

During my journey as a boy preacher, many folks who had good intentions approached me many times and tried to talk me out of what I was doing. There was one time when a group of pastors and leaders in the Bible institute I was attending in San Jose Costa Rica, were so concerned for my welfare and childhood development that they approached me and questioned me intricately as to why I was studying the Bible and why I had quit school. At that stage, I had decided to put a stop to my studies and go to Bible institute for eight months as there was an intensive program happening at this institute. With my parents support and under God's leading, I chose to sit under the Apostles and Prophets whom from time to time came and taught us the Word. This was no light or entertaining Bible program but rather a very intense and profound one. I will always cherish the memories I have of this short season in my life, as God was training me for the intense ministry overseas that was set to commence after I graduated from Bible institute. After this incredible time and despite many challenges and criticism, I went ahead and together with my dad, we started traveling the nations! Sometimes you have to choose to listen to God above men because men may get it wrong from time to time. Never look for men's approval to begin the call of God in your life, but rather seek for His approval and then consequently He will give you favor with men!

A journey to conquer the mantle

Each place where Elisha went with Elijah on this journey is symbolic and it represents a prophetic season that marked his destiny. This narration in its entirety gives us an account of Elisha's visit to three strategic places before inheriting the double portion. Firstly, Elisha left Gilgal and followed Elijah to Bethel and that's how the journey started. Gilgal represents the beginning of Elisha's spiritual journey. There is more than one site named Gilgal in the Bible, but the first Gilgal was the location where the Israelites camped after God enabled them to miraculously cross the river Jordan. Gilgal literally means, "rolled," referring to God having "rolled away the reproach of Egypt" from His people (Joshua 5:9). It was also the site where all the Israelite males were circumcised, as they were born in the desert and belonged to a generation that had not yet been consecrated to God. In our own spiritual journey, Gilgal could represent the moment when we are set apart for God, when He cleanses us and sets us free from the reproach of our past (just as the Israelites were called out of the idolatrous nation of Egypt). It is the moment when we enter into a covenant with God by the shedding of Jesus' blood on the cross and commit to belonging to Him and giving our lives to His call. It is the place of commencement where God encounters you and sets you free. I will compare it to the experience of salvation, as this is the first experience any believer has in his or her own walk with God. However, many prefer to pitch their tent, so to speak, and remain in Gilgal, meaning they remain in that spiritual level and never aspire for anything beyond salvation. As we know, being saved is just one of the many unlimited blessings God will share with us in this life. Salvation is important and keeping it is even more relevant as the Apostle Paul said,

> "...continue to work out your salvation with fear and trembling," (Philippians 2:12).

Nonetheless, it is not the end of the journey but rather the first step into this glorious road. Many remain content with their salvation experience even though there is more that God wants to give them. Unfortunately, they may never experience it because they don't aspire to ask for greater things or they limit God because of their own fundamentalist theology. God never intended for his people to stay in Gilgal, but rather He wants his chosen ones to keep walking and discover the marvelous hidden treasures on this life expedition.

After Gilgal, Elisha set out to Bethel. The meaning of the Hebrew word Bethel is "House of God" or "Gate of Heaven." It was there that Jacob had the vision of the ladder and had a powerful encounter with his Creator. As a result of this divine appointment, Jacob's life was totally changed. It was necessary for Elisha to pass through Bethel before going to Jericho. In other words, it was necessary that Elisha have a life-changing encounter with God in order to pursue and develop His calling.

It is at Bethel where God shapes our character and molds us with His Presence; it is where our lives are transformed by His power and our communion with Him is taken to another level. It is necessary to pass through this process before entering the Promised Land. (The prophets were on their way to Jericho, the first city in the Promised Land that the Israelites took possession of.)

The length of this stage of our spiritual journey depends upon our obedience to God. Many times I have heard many Christians saying, "I am being tested." My question is, "When are you going to pass through the test and begin to enjoy all that God has prepared in Canaan for you?" By Canaan, I speak of the inheritance that God has promised you. I assure you that one of the factors that can accelerate the testing process in our lives is our obedience to God's call, that is, when we begin to do His will and not ours. When we begin to walk in His will, in His time and in the correct season, we will have success in all we do, in Jesus name. Bethel is a time of formation in anyone's walk with God. It is a place where He strips the old man off you and brings the new man, as the Scripture says in Ephesians 4:22-24,

> "You were taught, with regard to your former way of life, to put off your old self, which is being corrupted by its deceitful desires; to be made new in the attitude of your minds; and to put on the new self, created to be like God in true righteousness and holiness."

It's a place of the renewal of our minds and hearts; a land where He will change our spiritual names, thus affecting our legacy and destiny in the future.

This is precisely what happened to Jacob when he encountered God at Bethel. Jacob was in a terrible state as he had left everything behind, running from his brother, Esau, and fearing for his life. After Esau learned that Jacob took the blessing from his father, Isaac, he planned to kill Jacob once his father died. Jacob's fate could have been a lot worse if he hadn't met with God at the moment of his need. On his journey to Paddan Aram, fleeing from Esau, he found a place to rest where he had a dream which basically changed the outcome of his life's destiny (Genesis 28:12-15).

Conquering Jericho and crossing the Jordan

Once Elisha had left Bethel, the prophet went on to Jericho, the historic place of Israel's victory. In order to take the city, the people of God walked around its walls seven times. These walls were supposedly immovable and indestructible, the pride of Jericho City. However, God tore them down in a matter of seconds when a courageous nation, who had lived through a difficult time, dared to believe Him for a miracle. When we understand the purpose of our calling and begin to possess what God has promised us, then we can walk into our Jericho and tear down the walls that are impeding us from entering the Promised Land, as we take the plunder God has left us. It is imperative to follow His voice and obey him unconditionally during this time of conquest. Many believers, when they get to a high point in their life or ministry, ignore how much the enemy will try to push them backwards. One of the tactics the enemy can use is discouragement. An example of this can be seen when the enemy used the sons of the prophets to discourage Elisha from following Elijah.

Upon crossing the river, just as his ancestors had done many years earlier, Elisha was given what he had desired for so long, and it was there that he received and saw the fulfillment of his calling. If you want to obtain the mantle, you will have to get rid of any avarice, selfishness and greediness. Only those who are willing to go on this journey and who are courageous enough will get to the other side of the Jordan.

The Jordan River is no common river as it was the place where God's supernatural power was displayed on many occasions. I could recite many stories in this book about events that took place at the Jordan River. One of them was the official bestowal of God's anointing upon Elisha. Before he was officially anointed by God, he was asked by his mentor to see him before he was taken away or else it wouldn't happen (2 Kings 2:10). Make no mistake, Elijah never transferred the mantle on to his successor Elisha. In fact, he was carrying the mantle up until the point when he was separated by the chariots of fire and departed in a whirlwind. The Bible says that the mantle dropped onto the ground as Elijah was being taken to heaven. Elisha, mesmerized by the amazing sight of God's supernatural realness, walked forward where the mantle was, picked it up, and the rest is history! He was anointed by heaven and only God Almighty transferred such an incredible and great anointing to one of His trustworthy friends, "Elisha."

There is a popular saying among many Christians when they see an anointed person – "If I could just hang out with the prophet I could have some of that anointing rubbed on me." It's not as easy as hanging out with the anointed one and catching the mantle. The fact of the matter is, that if you want to pursue the greatest gift of the Holy Spirit, "The Anointing," it's going to take more than spending hours hanging out with your pastor, mentor, or leader. You will have to make an individual decision to build a solid and lasting relationship with Jesus. Just as Elisha was intentional about his goal, you must be too! God wants to take you to the other side of the Jordan. It has always been his desire since the day you started this walk with Him.

The Jordan River is not just a closing chapter place, but on the contrary, it's just the beginning of a great adventure between you and God. I see this spiritual and prophetic place as the place of your graduation, but as we all know, it doesn't finish there. No one is successful by attending a prestigious college and hanging their certificate on the wall. You become successful the day you start practicing and doing what you devoted so much of your life to. This principle obviously applies to people who are passionate about what they do and what they have studied. It is sad that, unfortunately, many people waste their time in trying to do something they never felt passionate about, and even though they graduate, most of them don't end up working in the profession in which they majored in. It is the same with the call of God on your life. Unless you are passionate about it and start using the mantle He has given you, then the time spent at a Bible college or seminar profits little, as God doesn't require you to have multiple certificates or degrees. Knowledge is good, but if that knowledge is not used for the ministry or talent He has given you, then that knowledge is merely "head knowledge." It won't really take you anywhere in your calling unless you activate your call by stepping out and making an impact in your generation!

The first thing Elisha did when he picked up the mantle

was to fold it in half and strike the waters just as he saw his mentor do just hours earlier. Elisha had to take a step of faith and believe God for the supernatural and that's when his ministry started. It takes a step of faith in God's timing to move in the right direction and follow His footsteps. We are called to be catalysts of revival and bring change to our communities, and the only way we will achieve this is by stepping out, moving forward and walking towards His place of destiny for our lives and families.

Chapter 16

Activate Your Calling

I remember the first time I was invited to preach at a connect group meeting. I was only nine years old, passionate for the Lord, and recently had been healed of a deadly tumor between my lungs and my heart. All I wanted to do around that time was tell my friends how much Jesus loves them. I began to get ready for the call of God by being very creative in my preparation time. When I look back and think of the things I did as a child, even though I am now only 28 years old, I giggle to myself, thinking that I was so on fire for Jesus that I wanted to get everyone saved, even my own toys. My passion grew to such a crazy degree of holy insanity that I would lock myself in my room in the afternoons after school and play revival meetings with my toys. I would lay hands on them and reenact the whole meeting. I so wanted to serve the Lord that I was bursting from the inside to preach the gospel. My parents were so concerned about my behavior that they decided to take me to see a psychologist. Oh friends, I can tell you that was the best evangelistic session of my life. Yes, I witnessed to the specialist too and at the end of a long chat with this guy, he finally gave up and called my parents. What he said changed the course of how they would view my passion for ministry in the years ahead. The call of God came upon my life at a very young age but I knew that if I didn't do anything about it, I would never walk in it as in my family there were no preachers. My dad was the owner of two bars in the community, and from time to time, I would sneak out and preach to his clients about Jesus. My dad would get so mad that he would send me back home. He was afraid that I would scare the clients with my "Gospel thing." What he didn't realize was that my mother and I had been praying for the bars to shut down for a while and God supernaturally shut down his business. Years later, after God dealt with him and stripped everything from him, he decided to surrender his life to Jesus. God had to do something supernatural to get this boy from a small country town in Alajuela, Costa Rica, to the platform of the nations. However, it wasn't an easy journey as there were many great and not so great chapters where I learned many things. It was my passion to step out in faith that was the initiator to get me started. Obviously God was in it and He was the one opening the doors, but if it weren't for God's supernatural favor and for the "I want to preach now" attitude, I would have never started at such a young age; perhaps I would have started years later. The fact is that the calling was there and many prophets, when they came to my home church, recognized it. They knew God had called me to the nations to preach the gospel. Nonetheless, it took many steps of faith and action to see those prophecies come through. Some folks believe that when God gives you a prophetic word that's it, and there is nothing to be done about it, that it would be done in God's timing and that it would require no action on their part. Let me tell you, dear friends and readers, that having this kind of thinking will delay your process in getting started. If God has already spoken, all you have to do is activate the word by taking dramatic steps of faith towards your growth in the calling and the ministry He has promised you.

Chapter 17

Dreamers and Conquerors

Joseph's life came to a crossroad when he was thrown into an empty well in the fields of Shechem because of a dream. Hours later, his brothers sold him to a caravan of Ishmaelite merchants, who were going to Egypt, for twenty pieces of silver, as the account of Genesis 37 tells us. Days after, Joseph "The Dreamer" found himself serving in the house of Potiphar, an official of Pharaoh. It was there that he gained favor before all and God blessed him, changing him from being a Hebrew slave to Potiphar's most trusted man. In the midst of all this, the enemy rose up against Joseph by putting an evil suggestion in the mind of Potiphar's wife. She fully embraced it and began to pursue the young man relentlessly each day, trying to persuade him to sleep with her. In the face of temptation however, when Potiphar's wife put her hands on Joseph and tried to persuade him to sin against God, he fled and ran outside. Joseph was a man who chose to be loyal to the Lord rather than give up his prophetic destiny and risk sacrificing his intimacy with God. Although he had already lost his coat of many colors when he was sold as a slave (Joseph's brothers stained it with goat's blood and then presented it to their father, claiming he had been killed by a wild animal), he had never surrendered the prophetic destiny that his coat represented. In the Bible, a coat, or mantle, is often representative of authority, or coming under someone's protection. For example, Ruth came to Boaz on the threshing floor to ask if she could come under his mantle (Ruth 3:1-9). Both of them knew that according to the customs of the day, if Boaz literally put his mantle over Ruth then this act would symbolically show his willingness to take her as his wife. Ruth would belong to him, come under his protection and be brought into his household to have her life bound up in covenant with him in marriage. She would be coming under his headship and authority as a husband. The mantle, being symbolic of authority, is also evident as we have seen in the story of Elisha and also in Isaiah 9:6 where it was prophesied of Christ:

> "For to us a child is born, to us a son is given, and
> the government will be on his shoulders..."

Taking into account the Biblical significance of a mantle, we begin to see that even though Joseph was in slavery, his coat represented the calling that was irrevocably on his life (see Romans 11:29). The fact that he was set apart for God, that his life was to be bound up in God's will and overseen by His protection and that he carried Godly authority upon his shoulders, never left him. That is why, even when he was in slavery, he prospered! I am not talking about financial prosperity here, but rather the greater prosperity of walking in God's divine purpose and in the gifts that He has given you. Everything under Joseph's care flourished (Genesis 39:3-4), as he exercised the gifts God had given him.

Where your gifting is, favor also follows, as happened to Joseph. He was gifted with excellent administrative and leadership skills, and Potiphar recognized this. Soon this "slave" had others under his authority – you could take the dream coat from the man, but you couldn't take the dreams and the prophetic destiny out of the man, so to speak! To be a conqueror and step into the dreams God has for you, you must be willing to embrace hardship, but all the while, understanding that what God has planted inside of you cannot be snatched away. While feeling weak, you still have God's authority, and while feeling like you are a dimly flickering light, the gifts God has put inside of you burn brighter than ever. Only wait patiently and do not lose hope. Keep your eyes fixed on God and what He has promised you, not the circumstances that surround you. Something that will help you do this will be your attitude to suffering. Do you see hardships as opportunities for God to refine you and grow the gifting he has sown in you? Also, know who you are in God, no matter where you are. There is a story about an officer in the army and a group of soldiers under his command who were captured and kept in a POW camp during World War II. During their time in the camp, the officer continued to look after his men, putting them before himself in many cruel situations. Eventually, the officer and his men were able to make an escape from the concentration camp and were found by their fellow British troops, wandering through the forest, exhausted from their flight. When asked his name, the officer first stated his rank then his name. It is clear from this story, that even while in prison, nothing changed the fact of who this man was. His rank, position, experience and responsibilities towards his men were not forgotten, even in the most nightmarish of places. He knew who he was before, during and after being in the camp – his environment could not take that away from him. So must our identity in God be and the surety we have of the calling he has placed upon our lives.

So it was Joseph's fear of and faith in God which sustained him while he was in jail for two plus years. Even in his time of imprisonment however, God continued Joseph's training, preparing him to be the most powerful administrator in the whole land at a critical time in the Egyptian empire's history. Upon reading Joseph's biography carefully, we can come to the conclusion that as a great visionary, he also had to pay a great price. In spite of this, Joseph never gave up and always maintained his firm conviction in the Lord. His heart completely sold out to God, Joseph walked in obedience and in blessing wherever he went, willing to take the time necessary to go through God's processes in his own life.

Over the years, I have had people approach me with the same question on numerous occasions, asking, "What can I do so that God will fulfill my dream?" Dear friends, God has a blessed habit, and it is to make the dreams of his children a reality. He is a God who walks with dreamers and blesses them greatly. There are crucial moments in our lives that we go through when we feel as though the seeds that were planted within us so long ago are simply dreams which will never be made concrete. There is a great reality however, and it is that God changes these difficult moments into opportunities, making them into a pathway leading to the fulfillment of desires that have been in our hearts for many years. In such times, we must remember therefore God's enduring promises to us:

"What I have said, that will I bring about, what I

have planned, that will I do." (Isaiah 46:11b)

And ,"so is my word that goes out from My mouth;
it will not return to me empty, but will accomplish
what I desire and achieve the purpose for which I
sent it." (Isaiah 55:11)

Knowing that God is the Lord who always fulfills what
He has spoken helps us to not lose heart or become discouraged.
In the words of an old adage, "God said it, I believe it, and that
settles it!" I believe that the heart of God is saddened many times
by our lack of trust in Him. If we simply hold on to His Word,
bearing in mind that what He promised He would fulfill, what
He has spoken to us will come to pass. If the dreams that God
has given us are truly Biblical, God-given and God-inspired,
they must come to pass. As surely as the law of gravity says
that if we throw a ball up in the air, it will come back down, in
the same way, when God said, "Let there be light," nothing in
the universe could hold back that event from occurring. It was
instantly irreversible and as the uttered Word of God, it had to
come to pass. As the Word of God also says,

"God is not a man, that he should lie, nor a son of
man, that he should change his mind. Does he speak
and then not act? Does he promise and not fulfill?"
                                            (Numbers 23:19)

This is one of God's principles I have seen Him operate
time and time again in my life.

During a very exciting stage of my life, having recently
become engaged, as my wife and then fiancée Rebekah can testify,

the journey for us to get married was a tremendously difficult one. It involved a long distance relationship from different continents and different sides of the world over the course of three arduous years. We travelled back and forth between America (where I resided back then) and Rebekah's homeland, Australia, whenever possible. However, there was one time when we were not able to see each other for a whole year due to some visa and calendar issues. During this time however, it was the promises, those vivid dreams and revelations that God impressed upon us so powerfully in the early days of our relationship, that enabled us to stay strong in Him and not lose hope. Although there were times when confusion attacked us and the circumstances seemed overwhelming, the roots of the dream God had planted inside of us, the promise of being husband and wife, went too deep to be uprooted. Once God utters a dream for your life, He will bring it to pass. All that we must do is believe Him, take Him at His word and be willing to go through whatever is necessary to see it come to fruition. Just as a butterfly, which emerges from its cocoon without a struggle, the dreams of God must pass through a process in order to survive and last the distance. Isaiah 48:10 speaks of this process we must pass through: "See, I have refined you, though not as silver; I have tested you in the furnace of affliction." When we come out of "heated" situations, it is God's will that we emerge from the furnace with all impurities stripped away, such as pride, selfishness and immaturity which can rob us of the blessing of seeing God's will fulfilled in our lives.

Lastly, we must not think that the fulfillment of God's dreams depends solely upon us. God will fulfill His purposes irrespective of whether or not we decide to cooperate with Him, but whether He is able to use us to bring His heart's desires to pass is contingent upon our willingness. This is illustrated beautifully in a story that evangelist Reinhard Bonnke tells, when he recounts how God once revealed to him that before calling him, God had asked other men to answer the calling to go to Africa but they refused. Reinhard felt humbled, realizing that he had taken up a baton of ministry which had become his because others had refused to take hold of it. As a result of taking this baton and obeying God, Reinhard has been able to see the salvation of millions of souls in Africa and the whole world.

God is sovereign, and He will see His purposes through. Whether we decide to take up the privilege of being part of that is up to us.

God is the God of men and women who dare to dream great dreams. God seeks dreamers in whose hands He can place immense projects that will be for the blessing and expansion of His kingdom on earth. Joseph never imagined that Egypt would be the place where all his dreams would be fulfilled, right down to the letter. Strange or as illogical as it may seem to us, God prepared Joseph for his life's mission in a foreign household and a jail. He took him from being abandoned by his brothers all those years before, to being administrator over all the riches of the Egyptian empire in a time of severe famine. In spite of everything that happened in his life, Joseph was not dismayed and kept up his faith and conviction until the end.

Although sometimes the ways in which God operates may seem irrational or incomprehensible to us, we must remember His declaration in Isaiah 55:8-9:

> "'For my thoughts are not your thoughts, neither are
> your ways my ways,' declares the LORD. 'As the

heavens are higher than the earth, so are my ways higher than your ways and my thoughts than your thoughts.'"

God works in mysterious ways, and as His friends and as dreamers in His kingdom, we are not meant to question Him but rather to obey Him. Do not insert a question mark when God puts a period; God is the only one who has the answer and He will help you understand it in His due time. Rather, we should occupy ourselves in pleasing Him all our days and in seeking His kingdom; in being obedient to fulfilling the commission that He has given us. If we do this, He will take care of the rest, including the desires of our hearts:

"But seek first his kingdom and his righteousness, and all these things will be given to you as well." (Matthew 6:33)

Chapter 18

What to Do When You Have a Dream and How to Fulfill It

The question is then, what should you do when you have a dream or a great project that God has put in your heart? Over the years, God has taught me four steps that I would like to share with you in this chapter.

1. Confess the dream God has given you

The Scriptures teach us that there is power in our confessions. For this reason, the Apostle James insisted we be careful with our words (see James 3:1-12). Confessing our dreams is a way of activating them in faith and believing that God will fulfill them. It is necessary, however, to ensure that we share our dreams with other visionaries. In this way, we will be built up by each other's encouragement rather than become disheartened by negative counsel. If you share your dreams with the wrong people, the enemy can try and take advantage of the situation. This is how criticism arises, envy grows and disagreements can result. In such cases, we need to use the spiritual weapons of discernment and wisdom that God has given us.

Practically speaking, the gift of discernment in operation may look like this: Let's say there's someone with whom you desire to share the ideas God has given you, but you are unsure of whether you should proceed. We may begin at times like this to "test the waters," that is, to share perhaps part of the vision with them to see if there is a favorable response. If there seems to be no negative feedback, the temptation is to go on what we see outwardly and hear from that person, rather than asking God for the revelation of what is really going on, spiritually speaking. It could be that there is an unseen door in the person's life whom you are speaking to which could be open to jealousy or envy, resulting in their criticism. That door will not be visible to you, of course, and this is why you must ask the Holy Spirit to make known to you what hindrances there may be to sharing the dreams God has given you. God speaks to us differently, but generally if you have a sense of hesitation (even though your mind may be saying, "What's the problem, we have the all clear here, it's going to be fine! Look, they are responding positively," or, "They are my family/close friend. Of course they are going to accept and support what God has shown me"), you still need to inquire further if it really is a wise idea to proceed. If the uneasiness continues, wait and pray for further instructions or decide not to share at all, based on the Holy Spirit's leading. If the uneasiness is purely on your part, through prayer, the Holy Spirit will remove it and give you the peace to share. One final word of caution here: Do not assume that those closest to you, particularly your family, will automatically understand the dreams God has given you. Sadly, there is a story repeated time and time again in the Bible, that the enemy often rises up members of a person's family against them in order to stop their God-given dreams from coming to pass, as was the case with Joseph, Jeremiah, and many others. The reason for this is because the enemy knows that the people of greatest influence, and the ones we have the greatest emotional ties with, may have a great impact on our lives when giving their advice.

A dream is like a newborn baby – we must protect and nurture it, not expose it to inspection and criticism by all. Imagine how you would feel if someone made a critical comment about your precious newborn infant! This is how God feels when we unwisely toss around the dreams He has given us to be criticized by anyone who chooses. We must show that we can be faithful in guarding the dreams that God has given us, bearing in mind:

> "Whoever can be trusted with very little can also be trusted with much, and whoever is dishonest with very little will also be dishonest with much."
>
> (Luke 16:10)

God longs to share with us the desires and dreams of His heart to a greater and greater degree, but we must be able to show Him that we can be trusted with the revelations He gives us; that we will not boast about what we received or use the knowledge we have been given unwisely. For example, can you imagine how reluctant a husband would be to have a deep and transparent conversation with his wife if he felt that she was going to repeat his words the next day to her friends? It is the same in our relationship with our Heavenly Father. God will only reveal to us the deep secrets of His heart when He knows we will not be careless with what He entrusts us.

Do not allow those who disagree with your vision to discourage you, much less to stop you from fulfilling God's purpose for your life. It is necessary to continue to proclaim and pray for the desire of your heart, and in doing so, "birth" the dreams of God for your life.

This can be likened to when a mother-to-be is in the final month of her pregnancy. She speaks continually about her child; her heart's greatest desire is to hold her newborn baby in her arms. In the same way, we should confess and dream with the covenant promises that God has planted in our spiritual wombs.

2. Overcome obstacles

We need to prophesy over our circumstances and speak in faith even when the outlook does not seem very promising. From when I was little, I always had the conviction that God had a great calling over my life, but I still had to face some "dream killers" who did not believe that God could call a child from such a young age.

I remember greatly enjoying praying and engaging in spiritual warfare; I would often put on my small radio and shut myself in my room. Once when I was just nine years of age, I remember praying for an hour, rebuking and binding in spiritual warfare. A neighbor, who was very worried by this situation, called my mother one morning, saying that so much spiritual warfare would cause the enemy to attack me, and also she felt, from the Lord, that my mother should advise me to stop. Being a new believer, my mom did not understand why our neighbor had made such a comment, and so one afternoon when a pastor was giving Biblical counsel on the radio, she decided it would be a good time to clear up any doubts. Immediately she dialed the radio station's number and mentioned the incident. I remember being in my room and able to hear the pastor's counsel, thinking, "God, I hope that my neighbor hears this exhortation." In simple terms, he said, "Tell this sister that the only one who should shut up is the enemy, because there is power in prayer." From that day, she did not return to make any more remarks about my prayer.

Another example of discouragement can be found in Numbers 13, the account of the Israelite spies sent into Canaan. At the end of forty days, they returned to the Israelite camp at Kadesh in the desert of Paran, giving Moses and Aaron their report and showing the fruit of the land they had brought back.

> "They gave Moses this account: 'We went into the land to which you sent us, and it does flow with milk and honey! Here is its fruit. But the people who live there are powerful and the cities are fortified and very large. We even saw the descendants of Anak there. The Amalekites live in the Negev; the Hittites, Jebusites and Amorites live in the hill country; and the Canaanites live near the sea and along the Jordan.'" (Numbers 13:27-29)

At times, we will have to face people and even ministries that present discouragement rather than encouragement to take possession of what God has promised us. Be encouraged however, and know that many godly men and women were faced with the dilemma of dealing with "narrow vision people" when others did not believe in what God was doing in their lives. The story of the spies sent out to explore the land of Canaan illustrates this well, particularly when opinions became divided between those who said, "There are giants and dangerous animals," and those who said, "Is not our God stronger than them?" Things came to a head when Caleb silenced the people before Moses and said,

> "We should go up and take possession of the land,
> for we can certainly do it." (Numbers 13:30)

Caleb had to confront those men of little revelation whom did not understand God's purpose and only saw and felt in the natural, the carnal and the tangible. On many occasions, we as visionaries are going to have to listen to a sole opinion, that of our dear and loyal friend, our Lord Jesus Christ. If we listen to what the dream killers tell us, it can be dangerous, even abortive. Do not allow anything or anyone to discourage you, distract you, or make you lose your focus. Walk beneath God's cloud and follow it, and the God of Abraham, Isaac and Jacob will show you His glory as you journey towards the Promised Land.

One other important thing to note concerning this area is, that sometimes even ministers do not recognize or acknowledge what God has placed in a believer's heart. In spite of this however, we must be aware, above all else, that we are not called by men, but rather, we have been chosen by God who has called us by His great mercy.

A word of caution here however: I am not suggesting that if people in positions of God-given authority in our lives do not recognize the dreams He has given us, that it gives us the right to fly in the face of authority. Sadly, there are many who go from church to church causing divisions, because they bitterly defend their dreams and fight vehemently against anyone they see as being "an obstacle." Remember when Peter tried to turn Jesus aside from His calling, Jesus did not rebuke Peter, but Satan, the spirit operating against the will of God. For this reason, Jesus told Satan, rather than Peter to get behind him. Even if people are in opposition to you, remember, our fight is not against flesh and blood (Ephesians 6:12). We must not attack people, but rather, pray against the spiritual forces trying to hinder God's will. Many times, people who discourage others do not even realize they are doing it. They think they are simply giving helpful counsel or giving "realistic" warnings. If your dream is of God, He will bring it to pass, regardless of whether those in positions of influence in your life believe in it or not. Knowing this prevents us from getting into conflicts and trying to defend ourselves in our own flesh. Rest in God. No one can convince others that your dream is really from Him – He alone can do this. However, having said that, you do not need the approval of man to validate the dream He has given you. There are also some situations when a season under particular leadership has ended, as God's favor has been withdrawn from that leader. You then can strike out in faith in order to see a dream fulfilled as long as you are led by the Holy Spirit. If this were the case, I would advise you to firstly be absolutely certain that God is calling you out into a different place. Remember, God is your ultimate authority – if it comes down to a choice between following His Word or the counsel of man (no matter what the individual's position), you must be sure to obey God. As we mentioned previously, obedience is key to releasing your calling. Secondly, if you do feel led to move out, it would be wise to come out from discouraging leadership in (as much as possible) a respectful and loving way, by honoring your authority and blessing them as you leave.

> "With all lowliness and meekness, with long-suffering, forbearing one another in love; Endeavoring to keep the unity of the Spirit in the bond of peace." (Ephesians 4:2-3 KJV)

Thirdly, ask God to show you a new spiritual covering you can come under. It is important that you be accountable. There are no lone rangers in the kingdom of heaven. Even pastors of the largest churches in the world need someone they can call as a mentor, someone they can go to for counsel and encouragement. Ask God to give you wisdom, to guide you to the right spiritual leader or leaders who can support you in fulfilling God's call for your life.

One time I remember having to make the decision to leave a church covering that was controlling. It was very sad when it happened, as I had formed deep and meaningful relationships with people and even with the pastors. As the ministry began to grow and I was getting more and more invitations, my pastor noticed our absence in the church. Despite trying to remain plugged in to the church, there was a time when my father and I were traveling so much that we could hardly attend church anymore since our meetings were on the weekends. One time the pastor said from the pulpit, "If you are not on this bus and you are not heading where this bus is heading then the door is open for you to get off the bus." My mom and I felt deeply hurt by those words, as we knew the context of where he was coming from. Days earlier he asked my mom to take on a connect group and have me as a connect group leader. He manifested that he was deeply concerned for me and that we needed to slow down. Nonetheless, I knew that this leader was being driven by his own desire to grow his church, no matter what the cost was. He was trying to put ministers of the church in charge of connect groups. I didn't have a problem with leading a connect group, but at that time, I knew it was not the right season, and that I needed to spend all my energy and passion in growing the baby ministry God had entrusted me back in those days. Besides, I had a firm conviction that I wasn't called to minister in my local church, but that God had called me to win souls and minister to the wider body. After praying and going through the grief process of leaving the church, we immediately felt as if a burden was lifted off our shoulders. A few weeks later I met, at a Christian TV station, a leader who later on was going to become my pastor, my mentor and spiritual father. God used Pastor William Magana as a ministerial father who showed me the ropes, formed me and supported the vision God had put in my heart many years before I met him. After making the decision of attending Passion for Souls church, many things happened in our ministry that resulted in growing the ministry, not just nationally but also overseas. Many doors opened up as a result of obeying God and being under the right covering,

3. Following God's dream

To follow the dream that God has placed in us is one of the primary requirements to see it through, but it doesn't stop there. We then need to walk in line with our God-given destiny. Not only should we be dreamers, but we also need to be doers of our Heavenly Father's will. In this way, we will see the fulfillment of those dreams. It requires more than just confessing what we believe He will do. In order to enter into Canaan, He requires us to also take the steps of faith necessary to defeat all the obstacles present along the way. On various occasions, men and women of faith mentioned in the Scriptures, took radical decisions to walk in God's path. An example of one such circumstance was when Abraham had to leave his country and family without knowing where he was going. God had not shown him the precise place where he would be situated, but with firm faith and conviction he followed the Almighty (Genesis 12:1).

There are moments when we are going to have to make challenging decisions in order to advance in the perfect will of God for our lives. Remember, strive not only to have a dream or vision, but also strive to see its fulfillment. This is the time not only for us to dream, but also to take the steps necessary to enter into a new level. We should bear in mind as we do so that God is the only one who promotes us and brings us to the Promised Land; it is not by our own strength but by His Holy Spirit –

> "So he said to me, This is the word of the Lord to Zerubbabel: 'Not by might nor by power, but by my Spirit,' says the Lord Almighty." (Zechariah 4:6)

Furthermore, God will honor his children's obedience. If you walk in the direction the Spirit of God is taking you, it is certain you will reach the place of your destiny in less time than you think. Obedience accelerates the process and takes you to places where you had never imagined being. We should move when the cloud of His guiding presence moves and follow His plan to the letter. Leaving His will and walking in our own direction could cost us a very high price and set back the realization of our goals in Christ.

4. Activate the dream

God is faithful to fulfill the promises He has given us in our lives, as we have seen, but there is also a condition attached to this – we must activate these dreams by willingly stepping out in faith. Just as a landmine is not activated until it is stepped upon, our dreams will not be activated until we begin to walk in the direction God has called us. It is necessary to follow God's compass and walk in His will in order to enter the promised destiny He has for us. We must not simply "name it and claim it" as the popular Christian slogan has been, but also act upon the dreams God has given us, remembering that,

> "…faith by itself, if it is not accompanied by action,
> is dead." (James 2:17)

I strongly urge you, do not let fear hold you back! Step out of the boat as Peter did and walk towards Jesus and the destiny He has for your life. Do not be afraid of the risk of failure either! Many times, when we hear a sermon preached about Peter walking on the water, the emphasis is upon his "failure," when he became afraid and began to sink into the water. Yes, it is true that sometimes failures occur in our lives, particularly if we take our eyes off our Lord Jesus, but there is also another lesson to be learned here from Peter. Even though Peter grew afraid when he was on the water, he was actually quite courageous to even get out of the boat in the first place, something that none of the other disciples dared to do. Not only this, Jesus' invitation for Peter to come to Him on the water was preceded by Peter's bold request,

"Lord, if it's you...tell me to come to you on the water." (Matthew 14:28)

In a sense, it was as if Peter was unwittingly saying to Jesus, "Challenge me Lord, if that's you, if you really have the power to make me walk on the water too, move me out of where I am in my comfort zone and out into the unknown, closer to you." For us, the "boat" in our lives may represent our comfort zones, the everyday, the "norm," the routines we can become stuck in day in and day out. If you are living a life where you feel you are only half-living, may I suggest to you that perhaps you are not truly fully living, in the sense of fulfilling all that God has for you! There is more! God has a plan for your life – not only for your own sense of purpose and sense of fulfillment, but first and foremost, He has created a plan in mind for your life to touch the lives of others and draw you closer to Him.

I believe that in these last days God is calling His children to step out of our "boats" that keep us out of the turmoil and cold realities that the world is suffering. We must be willing to step out into the sea of humanity around us, willing to take the risk of experiencing the harshness of a dying world. In doing this, we will draw closer to the heart of Jesus for the orphans, the widows, the hurting, the poor and helpless. Much of the Word of God reads like a love letter to such people. If we truly have our hearts beating in time with His, we will love those He loves and be willing to have our hearts broken for the things that break His, such as injustice and oppression. Through loving them, we will know more of His love.

One more important point on this subject is that we don't

need to be afraid to fail, as God promises in Romans 8:28 (emphasis added),

> "And we know that in ALL things God works for the good of those who love him, who have been called according to HIS purpose."

The two key words I have highlighted here are ALL and HIS. Do you truly believe that God is able to use ALL things that have happened in your life and will happen for HIS purpose? If you do, then be not afraid as Jesus said to Peter, get out of the boat. Sometimes we can be so afraid of "missing God" that we actually do miss Him, in a big way. We miss out on seeing His promises fulfilled for us because we lose focus. If we keep our eyes fixed on Christ, it becomes quite hard to "miss him." If we, on the other hand, start focusing on our human frailty and ourselves, questioning our ability to hear from God, then there is a fairly large chance that we will miss Him. As James encourages us,

> "If any of you lacks wisdom, he should ask God, who gives generously to all without finding fault, and it will be given to him." (James 1:5)

Do you trust God enough to let Him guide you, trust Him enough that even if you miss His leading and begin to "sink" that He will reach out and take hold of you? We can step out onto the water with confidence, remembering God's promise to us in Isaiah 43:2a,b;

> "When you pass through the waters, I will be with

you; and when you pass through the rivers, they will not sweep over you."

If you have surrendered your life fully to Christ, if you have told Him that you are willing even to be uncomfortable to chase the dream He has for you, He will not let you drown, even if you make a mistake somewhere along the line. He will even turn these experiences around into lessons, which will serve you well in bringing you to the next level He has for you. This is the part of the refining process necessary to see the fulfillment of the dreams of God. For example, we see time and time again the tragedies that occur when young people in Hollywood achieve too much, too soon. If they do not have grounding for the success they achieve, it can actually destroy them. In the same way, if we are not willing to go through the refining process, there is the danger that we could begin to think that we brought about the dreams of God through our own strength, or we can even begin to glorify the dreams of God above Him. The fulfillment of His dreams in our life will always be to glorify Him and lift Him high. Whenever dreams seek to glorify an individual or a ministry, it is certain that the real focus has been lost – that of causing others to look to Christ and His glory. God can even glorify Himself through your failures – what a magnificent picture of God's love and steadfastness the disciples must have seen when they looked out onto the sea and saw Jesus pulling Peter up out of the water. Who knows, perhaps for Peter that experience may have even formed the basis of his personal revelation of who Jesus was when he declared in Mark 8:28; "You are the Christ."

Don't be afraid to step out. God will be glorified, both when you "walk on water" with Him (are walking in His divine will, in order to fulfill the dreams He has placed in you) and when you "sink" momentarily (misinterpret His will, become temporarily overwhelmed by the enormity of the task before you, etc.). I believe that one of the greatest weapons the enemy is trying to use to hold back and disempower the church today is fear.

The roots of fear go back to the fall. The original sin of pride (man agreeing with the enemy that somehow man could know better than God) resulted immediately in the birth of fear (when Adam and Eve hid from God). Adam and Eve did so because they at once experienced the separation from God that sin brings and the awful sensation of their vulnerability in being alone. Pride and fear are almost always linked. Fear looks away from trust in God and to our own ability to preserve ourselves. To trust in ourselves is pride. Although fear seems to be accompanied with a terrible sense of helplessness, there IS something we can do about it. If we allow God to work through situations when we feel afraid, fear actually has the potential to draw us closer to God. I am not saying that it should be a permanent fixture in our lives. It must be dealt with by the blood of Jesus and overcome, but fear can also cause us to cry out, "Lord I'm sinking, I need you! Lord you are the one who will reach out and catch me! Jesus you alone sustain me to walk on the water!" In this way, we will learn dependency upon God. Paradoxically to our human thinking, total divine dependency is the key to achieving great dreams in God. If we attempt things that are achievable only in our own strength, there is a good chance that such dreams are not of God.

If we dream of the impossible, in dreams which can be achieved in God alone, for His glory, then we can be certain we are on the right track!

Along this journey, there have been experiences God has given to me which I now recognize as being part of His blueprint for my life. They are events, some small, others more significant, in which I can see His divine fingerprint, even from when I was young. There have been many times on this journey that I have had to step out of the boat, out of my comfort zone, and obey God's voice. I wouldn't say it has been easy, but oh so very worth it. I wouldn't be where I am today in my life if I had stayed in the boat. Dear friend, my prayer is that He may give you the courage you need to "get out of the boat."

Chapter 19

A Soul-Winning Generation

In the month of Nisan in the twentieth year of King
Artaxerxes, when wine was brought for him, I
took the wine and gave it to the king. I had not been
sad in his presence before; so the king asked me,
"Why does your face look so sad when you are not
ill? This can be nothing but sadness of heart."

I was very much afraid, but I said to the king, "May
the king live forever! Why should my face not look
sad when the city where my fathers are buried lies
in ruins, and its gates have been destroyed by fire?"

The king said to me, "What is it you want?"

Then I prayed to the God of heaven, and I answered
the king, "If it pleases the king and if your servant
has found favor in his sight, let him send me to the
city in Judah where my fathers are buried so that I
can rebuild it."

Then the king, with the queen sitting beside him,

asked me, "How long will your journey take, and when will you get back?" It pleased the king to send me; so I set a time. (Nehemiah 2:1-6)

Nehemiah, the cupbearer, served the King each day with enthusiasm, even though he had been a victim of the great Israelite exile to Babylon. One day his friends brought him news of the lamentable things that were happening in Jerusalem. When Nehemiah entered the palace one afternoon to serve, the king noticed sorrow in the young cupbearer's face that he could not hide. When the king inquired why his heart was saddened, Nehemiah responded by telling of all that had happened to Jerusalem and its walls.

What impacts me the most about this man's story is that he went from being a cupbearer to becoming a general who would direct one of the greatest projects of his time; to reconstruct the walls of his native city. The young Nehemiah also had a passion for his people, so much so, that it even showed on his face. He did not just pray for them however, but he had a plan revealed to him by God to restore what the Babylonian armies had destroyed. With this project in mind, he requested of the King, letters to cross all borders and return to his homeland, as the Bible relates in Nehemiah 2:3-9.

God is calling forth a generation that not only cries out for souls but will also arise with a plan to rescue the lost. God seeks men and women who are passionate for the calling He has given them and who will carry out the strategies to achieve what they have dreamed of for many years. God used a missionary's invitation to a park to activate my calling when I was 11 years old, and in Nehemiah's case, it was his peers' report that ignited his heart to seek the rebuilding of his hometown. It did not take long before the young man arrived back in Jerusalem, as is told in Nehemiah 2:11-12.

Nehemiah so desired to see his city restored that he rose during the night and rode alone on horseback inspecting the walls. Undoubtedly, the reality was very difficult to face, but this fellow would not let anyone hold him back, not even Tobias, the Ammonite official, who later rose up to oppose him. His goal was defined, his focus set, and no one could stop him.

For all the cities of that time, walls were a powerful defense mechanism against intruders, providing a sense of protection and offering a high place where the watchmen and guards could protect the city from the enemies. For this reason, the inhabitants of Jerusalem felt vulnerable with the walls down and a great sense of humiliation. Applying this to the reality we face today, it is sad to see how many of our cities have been invaded by the enemy's territorial spirits, taking up unoccupied spaces like plagues. As Nehemiah did, so are we to rise and reclaim these places for the kingdom of God, bringing forth one of the greatest revivals the world has ever seen. If God has given you a plan, this is the time to accomplish it and arise in Jesus name so that you can make a difference in your community. Certainly, we are in perilous times when many churches are not focusing on conquering the land they are called to conquer, but rather are concerned primarily about their own ministries. The lack of evangelists and evangelism in many churches is one of the leading causes why many churches are no longer functioning as they should. It is somewhat concerning when you see that the priorities of many mainstream churches are not necessarily focused on winning souls. Most churches have become focused on entertaining programs to create a comfortable environment to increase their congregation. What we don't realize is that most churches that are inward focused are growing because of transfer growth but not because of new converts being added to the fellowship. It is necessary instead that we work in a spirit of cooperation, laboring to the end of winning as many souls for Christ. The only way to see these broken souls come into our churches and have an encounter with God is by shifting our focus and making it our goal to support, cherish, and send out the local church evangelists to the streets, shops, and the market place. Souls are the heartbeat of our Father and until we realize how vital it is for us as believers and leaders to become soul winners and disciple makers, then we will not see genuine growth in our churches and in the kingdom of God. We must be kingdom minded in order to achieve this goal and we also must be soul-winning minded. It is essential for many churches and church leaders to wake up to the reality that newcomers are not going to walk into your church and come to Jesus on the first Sunday service they attend, unless of course, there is a legitimate move of God in your ministry. It's imperative for us to raise the awareness of how important and how profitable it is for the kingdom when we support evangelism. Evangelism is close to His heart and if you love Him you would want to make Him happy! There is nothing in this world that makes our heavenly Father happier than seeing new souls coming into the gates of His kingdom! Winning souls is wisdom and is the call of every believer. You may say, "But wait a minute, I am not an Evangelist." You don't have to be! It is as simple as that. You need to realize that not everyone plays the role of an Evangelist in the kingdom; nonetheless we all play the role of winning souls.

Soul winning has been my greatest passion and hobby since I was a little boy. During school days I was given a nickname, "little priest," and that was because I used to witness to all my school friends during school recess. I wasn't shy about it and because of my compelling desire to tell my friends about Jesus, I used to get in trouble every now and then, since some of my friends and teachers weren't able to cope with the "boy preacher" telling them every day to repent and get right with God. One time after school was finished, I left the school premises and went to the bus stop where I would normally wait for my sister. However, this day my sister forgot she had to meet me there and she went straight home. When she got home, she realized that she had left her younger brother waiting at the bus stop. She told me she was so scared that day, and that she didn't want to face my mother and tell her what happened, as she was afraid she was going to get disciplined for it. Later on, she told me how mad my mom was and what a reprimand she got for leaving me waiting at the bus stop. Even though it was a mistake, as she frankly admitted it and felt so bad about it, my mom wasn't a happy camper at all. While waiting at the bus stop, I noticed that my sister wasn't coming. After waiting for ten minutes, I decided to approach this lady who was a stranger to me. Even though I had been warned by my mother to never approach strangers, nor get a ride with them, I thought it would be a good idea to strike a conversation with this lady as I waited for the bus to go home. After I broke the ice, so to speak, and asked how she was doing, I realized that she was a very friendly lady. I felt prompted to share with her about Jesus and so for the next twenty minutes, I poured my heart out and told her everything I knew about Jesus,

His love and the plan of salvation. After that, I led her to receive Jesus Christ as her Savior. She happily accepted my invitation and so I proceeded to pray for her. After I got through, she was so excited that she gave me a hug and put some coins in my hand and whispered in my ear saying, "This is for you to buy some snacks for the road." God amazingly arranged that, as one of the problems I was facing was not having money to pay for the bus fare. In fact my plan B was to tell the driver that when I got home I would pay him. However, God knew my predicament and blessed me for my step of faith in stepping out and talking to this lady about her need for a savior.

Chapter 20

Kingdom Culture

We belong to a powerful kingdom and enjoy intimate fellowship with our King, but there is also one other essential element of being part of God's kingdom. We are also called to be kingdom laborers. This means that we not only have the privilege of being part of the kingdom, but we also have the honor of working as one body in Christ for his kingdom's advancement. We are to advance the kingdom by using every resource available to us to take "The Message" to every corner of the world. However, we can't be part of something unless we know how it functions, and in order to understand how the kingdom works, we must know the kingdom's culture. Culture is something that has always fascinated me. I enjoy learning about different world cultures, the collection of customs, foods, habits, dress, ways of thinking, traditions, etc. These are the things that citizens of a country feel represent their nationality. Culture gives us a sense of belonging and an ability to relate.

For instance, in my home country of Costa Rica, we love the famous national dish "Gallo Pinto" for breakfast every morning. This is a dish which consists of mixed rice and beans.

Although it may sound more like a lunch or dinnertime meal, it is actually served for breakfast most of the time. As far as local cuisine goes, this is well known in Central America, and with all pride, I can say that Costa Ricans make the best Gallo Pinto ever! Now, just as Costa Rica and all countries have their own foods and identifying characteristics, so the kingdom of God also has a specific culture. The citizens of His kingdom will be known by demonstrating kingdom culture. This means that we are not to eat, talk, work, relate to others and live foremost according to the cultures of the world we live in, but rather, according to the culture of His kingdom which we build on earth by living as kingdom citizens. Sadly though, there is often reluctance among many believers to fully embrace the new identity and culture that God has given us. This is because, in order to understand kingdom culture, we need to understand the character of its King. Often we fail to be able to live as kingdom citizens because we do not truly know our King or we have false perceptions of Him. Religion encourages us to see God as angry, punishing and distant, rather than a deeply caring, tender and compassionate Father. It is true that God is also powerful, just and absolutely holy, but if we remove His tender loving attributes from the picture, the result is a distorted and incomplete image. With such an image, it is likely that we would end up "living for God" with actions motivated by fear rather than reverent, adoring love.

Once we begin to truly know God, aspects of kingdom living, such as prayer, fasting, worship, tithing and warfare, become a delight to us rather than a burden. As we live according to the original pattern that we are spiritually designed for, we will be changed even to our very core and our relationship with God will consistently grow and flourish.

What many of God's people have failed to see for so long is that a religious, traditional, dogmatic prayer lifestyle cannot keep the fire alive in our relationship with Him. When praying becomes a routine for you – watch out! You could be losing your first love. Remember, that when you see prayer as a sacrifice, rather than an offering you delight to bring, it will be twice as hard for your flesh to bow and do it. Prayer is meant to be the gift of direct communication with God, a privilege for us to enjoy as His children. As the psalmist David said,

> "better is one day in your courts than a thousand elsewhere..." (Psalm 84:10)

Chapter 21

A Kingdom Generation

Nehemiah was a brave man in never showing any signs of fear and always acting courageously. He was a man that walked in God's kingdom principles and who listened to God's voice above his own, even when the circumstances were not the best. He never took the challenge for granted and was a man that went after his goal to the point of fulfillment. One of his many values was his passion to get the job done. His drive to see a whole city restored and rebuilt was what kept him going even when some of the locals came against him. Nehemiah was a man that wanted to please his heavenly Father in everything he did.

As friends of God, we are also citizens of His kingdom and coheirs with Christ. It is therefore vital for the church to learn about its identity as kingdom people. One important point I would like to highlight in this chapter is that in order to advance as the church, we must have a kingdom mentality. Jesus spoke about the kingdom in most of His parables. In fact, the word "kingdom" appears in the four gospels forty times, as it was relevant and important for Him to leave a kingdom culture established among His own disciples. As we transition from the traditional church approach to a kingdom one, even our very way of thinking must change. We are no longer bound to a religious lifestyle but we are committed to an intimate and personal relationship with the King of kings.

The church must realize that Jesus wants to restore our true identity as the princes and princesses of God that we are. When we talk about the terms princes and princesses, we are not just referring to figures like those we might find in an animated children's movie, or titles that boost our self-esteem. Rather, we are referring to an army of royalty who knows their true identity in Christ, and is thus equipped with His power to stand against the tide of wickedness threatening to engulf humanity.

We must seek Him first, trust Him, and act according to kingdom conduct if we want to succeed in all we determine to do.

For so long, the enemy has been strongly opposed to this new revelation God is revealing to His church. He has tried to mislead people by the misinterpretation of what it truly means to be a kingdom citizen. When you grasp the whole revelation of what Christ meant when He said, "The kingdom of heaven is near." (Matthew 10:7), your prayer life will change, your mindset will be revolutionized, and your appetite for the Lord's Word will be even greater.

The Pillars of the Kingdom

The Word of God says:

"The Spirit of the Sovereign Lord is on me, because the Lord has anointed me to preach good news to the poor. He has sent me to bind up the broken hearted, to proclaim freedom for the captives and release from darkness for the prisoners, to proclaim the year of the Lord's favor and the day of vengeance of our God, to comfort all who mourn." (Isaiah 61:1-2)

Here we see four vital aspects of Jesus' ministry. His mission involved (1) preaching the gospel, (2) healing the broken hearted, (3) setting the captives free, and (4) proclaiming God's favor. As we are also called to do what Jesus did, these mandates also become our mandates; they are therefore part of kingdom culture. These four areas could also be summarized as: (1) salvation, (2) healing, (3) freedom, and (4) prosperity. These outline the areas that He desires for us and also wants us to bring to others. This is the foundational teaching of the kingdom and what I call "The four kingdom pillars."

In order to understand what His kingdom is all about, we need to open our minds and our hearts to these elemental principles. In order to be kingdom citizens, we must accept Jesus into our hearts and embrace His healing promise for us so that we live a healthy lifestyle in all aspects. By healing I don't just mean physical healing but also spiritual healing. In order to enjoy the benefits of the kingdom of God, one must open their heart to healing and forgiveness through Jesus' redemptive blood. As we walk in healing, then we will be able to experience freedom in many areas of our lives. Jesus' desire is for us to be free and free indeed! In order to commence this journey of discovering who you are as a kingdom citizen, we must let go of the past and embrace the new. This won't happen unless there is genuine healing and deliverance. This will take us to a path of prosperity, and when I talk about prosperity, I am not just talking about money but rather a holistic view on prosperity. The only way we can be prosperous is once we have reached the fullness of understanding our identity as children of God, embracing our healing and walking in complete freedom through His precious blood.

God desires us to benefit from the lifestyle that He always intended for us. He first and foremost wants us to know Him as our personal Savior, but this is just the beginning. We need to remember that we are not only adopted as His sons and daughters, but that the next step is for us to be heirs.

> "...You received the Spirit of adoption by whom we cry out, 'Abba, Father.' The Spirit himself bears witness with our spirit that we are children of God, and if children, then heirs – heirs of God and joint heirs with Christ, if indeed we suffer with Him, that we may be glorified together." (Romans 8:15-17 NKJV)

How amazing! We are coheirs with Christ! His inheritance has also become ours! Isaiah 61 shows us what that inheritance is – that just as Jesus was, so are we called to an inheritance of a mighty harvest of souls ("preach good news to the poor"), to see miracles, the supernatural power of God manifested ("... to heal the brokenhearted"), to see people's lives transformed as they are set free by the Holy Spirit ("to proclaim freedom to the captives"), and to a life of soul prosperity ("to proclaim the acceptable year of the Lord...to give...the oil of joy for mourning"). We are called to administer these aspects of the kingdom of heaven and also have the privilege of walking in them ourselves. In other words, we inherit salvation, healing, freedom and prosperity. Imagine for a moment a child adopted into a family who takes on the family surname. How strange it would be if the child refused to participate in any of the family traditions, anything that the family enjoyed doing for fun, or going on any of the usual family vacations. It is the same when we take the name of Christ but do not fully embrace the kingdom lifestyle, which is a reflection of our heavenly adoption. Many of us do this however, settling for accepting Christ but without ever entering into the fullness of all that He has intended for us. This is a terrible tragedy to settle simply for salvation alone; this could be likened to being given a shiny brand-new appliance and never even plugging it in, or to a hospital being given a wonderful state-of-the-art piece of medical equipment but never using it.

Once we accept Christ, we begin to bear His Name and we are known as "Christians." Just as the names of different nationalities are used, for example: Macedonian, Indian, Singaporean, Australian, American and Costa Rican, etc., and indicates where a person is from, the name "Christian" indicates that we originated from Christ. Therefore all our ways should be a reflection of the One we came from. I am not saying that we should be striving to live according to Christian pop culture, going with the flow of every feel-good doctrine that arises. For example, many times we have been taught a version of the faith message that waters the power of faith down to a matter of positive thinking. The difficulty with such teaching is that it is not fully Christ focused. The danger of divorcing faith from dependence on God is that if we declare something in faith of our own desires, apart from God's will, and it doesn't occur, what then? Will our eyes still be firmly fixed on Him, the "author and finisher of our faith"? (Hebrews 12:2) Will we have the same faith that Abraham had, faith so great in God's promises that he was willing to sacrifice his only son? Sacrifice is a necessary part of having faith. For faith to activate the awesome plans God has for our lives in their fullness, we must first be willing to lay down our will for His sake, saying as Jesus did "not my will Father but yours be done." (Luke 22:42) The reason that both Jesus and Abraham were able to have so much faith in God in the face of hardship is because they knew God; therefore they were able to fully trust in His power. That is how "Jesus, for the joy that was set before him, endured the cross" (Hebrews 12:2), and Abraham, whose faith was credited to him as righteousness "reasoned that God could raise [Isaac] from the dead." (Hebrews 11:19, emphasis added) Abraham and Jesus (being fully human) both had an attitude that said, "I don't like the look of the prospect before me. I can see this is going to cost me dearly. If there is another way, I would take it, BUT, I trust you God. I KNOW who You are, Your character, Your desires, Your ways. I'm willing to pay the price because You have a glorious plan." That is why we must not disregard the last part of Romans 8:17 which says,

> "...[We are] joint-heirs with Christ, if indeed we suffer with Him, that we may also be glorified together." (NJKV, emphasis added)

Suffering is a necessary part of a faith-filled lifestyle, a lifestyle that holds on to the salvation, healing, freedom and prosperity which God intends for us. We can never purchase the promises of God by our suffereing, any more than a woman can earn the right to call her child hers by the agony she goes through to give birth to a precious baby. In the same way, suffering is many times part of the process which births, through faith, all that rightfully belongs to us. We must not be afraid of it, but be willing to embrace it, just as Jesus embraced the cross. This calls for balance; we are not called to be a generation that constantly proclaims we are spiritually walking in the wilderness. To think we are always meant to have a suffering mentality can actually become fleshy, but to truly deal with suffering as God intends, causes us to draw closer to Him and to become more like Him.

I also feel, at this point, to add a word clarifying the definition of prosperity. Unfortunately, in some circles prosperity has become something of a dirty word, owing to its misuse. This does not invalidate in any way however, that prosperity is a very real aspect of God's will for us. We just need to understand what God has in mind when He thinks of prosperity. According to the Word, prosperity is not solely material. There is a deeper type of prosperity that is referred to, one that supersedes the material.

Note: The Bible does not say that we will never struggle financially, but rather, that in such circumstances, we can still know God's ultimate goal in prosperity, found in Philippians 4:12-13;

> "I know what it is to be in need, and I know what it is to have plenty. I have learned the secret of being content in any and every situation, whether well fed or hungry, whether living in plenty or in want. I can do everything through him who gives me strength."

Now, certainly the apostle Paul was a man who had a very close walk with God, a man of great faith. The question many ask is, "Was that faith failing him in some way that there were times in his life when he went hungry and was not living in financial abundance?" Certainly not! In fact, this type of walk, which embraces either end of the spectrum, has passed the greatest test of faith. An example of true faith is being in circumstances that seem bleak from an earthly outlook and yet saying, "God is my strength. He is my primary source of all I need. He sustains me." There is great power to be found in such faith in God. God wants you to realize that prosperity is not about the material blessings that will come to your life but rather is about you being prosperous in all areas of your life. This is what the Apostle John said about prosperity in 3 John 1:2:

"Beloved, I pray that you may prosper in all things
and be in health, just as your soul prospers." (NKJV)

Just as with the faith message, it is also possible to go from one extreme to another with the prosperity doctrine. We are not called to live with a poverty mentality either and fall into thinking that we must simply roll over and take financial hardship or believe that poverty comes from God. On the contrary, we need to speak in faith no matter what our circumstances are, recognizing that God is our Provider, our "Jehovah Jireh," and then rest in Him patiently, knowing that He will sustain us however He chooses.

Dear friends, the times in which we are living are not getting any easier. The reality is that many God-fearing, devout Christians are also struggling in our world's economic climate.

This is not because God has let us down. He desires that we be refined as gold, that we draw nearer to Him and therefore learn His true character, even when we happen to be in the furnace. Out of the furnace comes gold – a generation equipped in faith to go forth in humility and the power of the Holy Spirit to fulfill the great Commission, going "into all the world and preaching the good news to all creation." Also, seeing new believers added to the kingdom, casting out demons, speaking in new tongues, healing the sick, seeing miraculous signs and experiencing His supernatural deeds on earth. This is what kingdom culture is all about, living out and enjoying our Christian walk every day (Mark 16:15-18).

To do these things, as we said, is simply to walk in our true identity in Christ. It's who we are. We must daily seek His presence in order to be connected with Him and have our identity grounded in Him. We can only know who we are truly meant to be by knowing Him – after all, we are made in the image of God (Genesis 1:27). As we grow to know who we are in Him, His concerns become our concerns, His desires our desires. To follow His desires is to seek first His kingdom. If we do this, God promises He will provide for us (Matthew 6:33). What is required therefore, at the end of the day, is that we believe, accept, behave, and walk in our true identity as the body of Christ. Why behave? Sometimes, as God's people, we don't know how to behave in His presence, and instead of thanking Him for all His goodness, we complain about what happened that day, feeling the need to vent and tell God how terribly things went for us. What we need to do, however, when we come into His presence, is thank Him for all He has done. Then we proceed to worship Him. As we worship, we become aware of the Holy

Spirit drawing us near to God. It is not long thereafter that we are made ready to stand before our King. It is His very presence that escorts us into His glorious chambers.

Chapter 22

The Tabernacle Prayer Model

Many Christians don't realize the power in knowing how to pray and seeking God. My intention in this chapter is not to change your prayer lifestyle but to show you a better way to pray more successfully!

Apostle James is teaching on the power of prayer when he says,

> "... You do not have, because you do not ask God. When you ask, you do not receive, because you ask with wrong motives, that you may spend what you get on your pleasures." (James 4:2-3)

The problem for many believers is that they want the easy and quick method of prayer. Many feel disappointed because they feel like their prayers haven't been answered. The problem is not linked to whether your prayers are heard by God or not, but rather on how you approach the heavenly throne of grace. Many go into God's presence in the seeking help mode, telling the Father how bad they feel and what they have gone through during the day. After that, they go into the asking mode by listing all of their requests before God. See, the problem is not what you are doing but in the order of how you are doing it. God is your Father and your Friend, and as such, He would like to see you coming into His presence with thanksgiving before you even utter a word to request anything. In the days of the old covenant, the Israelites had to do numerous rituals in order to receive their forgiveness once a year. However, under the new covenant in which we live we are not limited by such protocol and all we need to do is surrender. During the process of old covenant worship, before the priests entered the Holy of Holies, they needed to offer an offering and present it before the Lord for the atonement of their sins. The way they presented an offering in those days was by sacrificing a baby lamb or goat, pouring the blood into a bowl and offering it to God. This was required since Jesus, "The Lamb of God," had not come yet and there was no other method of atonement but the sacrificial offerings.

Many years ago, during my first encounters with God, I learned the importance of what I call "The Tabernacle Prayer Model." This prayer pattern revolutionized my intimate time with my Creator. I would like to highlight three important aspects of this prayer model. We see these principles play a big role in the Old Testament worship according to the Scripture in 2 Chronicles 5:1-14:

> When all the work Solomon had done for the temple
> of the LORD was finished, he brought in the things
> his father David had dedicated—the silver and gold
> and all the furnishings—and he placed them in the
> treasuries of God's temple.

Then Solomon summoned to Jerusalem the elders of Israel, all the heads of the tribes and the chiefs of the Israelite families, to bring up the ark of the LORD's covenant from Zion, the City of David. And all the Israelites came together to the king at the time of the festival in the seventh month.

When all the elders of Israel had arrived, the Levites took up the ark, and they brought up the ark and the tent of meeting and all the sacred furnishings in it. The Levitical priests carried them up; and King Solomon and the entire assembly of Israel that had gathered about him were before the ark, sacrificing so many sheep and cattle that they could not be recorded or counted.

The priests then brought the ark of the LORD's covenant to its place in the inner sanctuary of the temple, the Most Holy Place, and put it beneath the wings of the cherubim. The cherubim spread their wings over the place of the ark and covered the ark and its carrying poles. These poles were so long that their ends, extending from the ark, could be seen from in front of the inner sanctuary, but not from outside the Holy Place; and they are still there today. There was nothing in the ark except the two tablets that Moses had placed in it at Horeb, where the LORD made a covenant with the Israelites after they came out of Egypt.

The priests then withdrew from the Holy Place.

All the priests who were there had consecrated themselves, regardless of their divisions. All the Levites who were musicians—Asaph, Heman, Jeduthun and their sons and relatives—stood on the east side of the altar, dressed in fine linen and playing cymbals, harps and lyres. They were accompanied by 120 priests sounding trumpets. The trumpeters and musicians joined in unison to give praise and thanks to the LORD. Accompanied by trumpets, cymbals and other instruments, the singers raised their voices in praise to the LORD and sang:

"He is good; his love endures forever."

Then the temple of the LORD was filled with the cloud, and the priests could not perform their service because of the cloud, for the glory of the LORD filled the temple of God.

1. Offering

The Holy Spirit taught me that in order for my prayer to be effective that I needed to offer myself as an offering before His presence. We need to understand the power of offering when we come into His presence; this is what is going to create the right atmosphere for the supernatural to happen. We surrender ourselves as an offering by disconnecting from our world of busyness and anxiety. What I recommend is that you set apart a time and a place to meet with the Holy Spirit on a daily basis and also that you develop a continual communing with the Lord, all through the day. There is power when we present ourselves as an offering before God, when we surrender and embrace

His presence, and when we let our world around shut down by walking into His world! You will never be the same when you learn the meaning of "offering." The best way to reach this level of surrender is by letting all distractions go. You will soon realize how cunning the enemy is by trying to distract you during the first few minutes of your prayer. This is what I call "breaking through the boundaries of your flesh by walking into the limitless place of His presence." Sometimes this will translate to turning your phone off or putting it on to vibration mode, letting your family know that you are going to seek the Lord and that you need their understanding, also, putting all of your tasks behind you by surrendering and submitting your mind to Christ! It is very important that you offer the best offering unto the Lord, meaning don't be half-hearted when you pray, but rather, fully and passionately seek Him with all your heart!

2. Worship

We see king Solomon inaugurating the temple and giving offerings unto the Lord. The Bible says that so many offerings came that Solomon could not record them or count them (2 Chronicles 5:6).

However, as it was accustomed, the offerings were presented before the Lord in a thanksgiving spirit and then the priests would present them and pour the blood of the sacrifice on the altar. As we look at this example of offering, they not only presented living sacrifices before the Lord but also worshiped, and their worship reached a height that the glory of the Lord saturated the temple and the priests couldn't remain standing because of the thickness of the presence of God (2 Chronicles 5:13-14). I love when that happens! It has happened to me on several occasions where the glory is so strong that it saturates the atmosphere, to the point where I have to grab on to the rail of the pulpit, as my knees become like jelly and my body trembles before the magnificent glory of the Lord!

God is not interested in your well-structured prayer or your eloquent words, but more so, He is keen on spending time listening to your pure and sincere worship. Heaven rejoices when the worshipers of the Lord elevate praise unto His name. I can imagine that most Sundays (since Sunday is the day that most churches around the world hold their worship services) heaven goes quiet for that whole day as worship is being poured out from every nation, tribe and continent in the world! Our heavenly Father delights in worship, so today I would like to encourage you that before you do anything during your prayer time, or even before you ask anything, that you spend time worshiping Him.

Worship is the heavenly passage to the next level and as you worship the Lord, you will notice that the atmosphere, wherever you are worshiping, will change drastically as the presence of God fills that place. Don't give up until the beloved Holy Spirit takes you to Jesus and Jesus takes you to the Father. That is the whole key to unlock this prayer model. If we look at the tabernacle or the temples built in those days, it had three sacred places: (1) the courtyards, (2) the Holy Place, and (3) the Holy of Holies. Jesus said that He is the way, the truth and the life and that no one goes to the Father except through Him. This is such a beautiful and heavenly designed way of worship. When I see those parallels I can see a deep revelation that unlocks the enigma of what worship is all about. The more you worship, the closer you will get to the Holy of Holies experience. If I can put it in practical terms, I would like to suggest that the Holy Spirit is the way, Jesus is the truth and the Father is the life. The Holy Spirit will show us the way, while Jesus shows us the truth and takes us to the Father, who will then breath life or the revelation of the supernatural into our lives. Remember when Jesus was asked by the disciples if they could sit at His right hand side, He responded that it was not for Him to assign those places of honor but for the Father. When we understand how beautifully united the trinity works, we can see that the three-in-one concept is not merely a concept, but that these three celestial beings, who are the only and true God, work in such harmony that it can be so deep and unfathomable to our human limited knowledge. This unity is once again confirmed in the pattern of the tabernacle. What Moses envisioned was a heavenly Tabernacle that is in heaven and that God allowed Moses to set up on earth. Every minor and major detail of the tabernacle reveals the grandness of the God of the trinity!

3. Thanksgiving

The Bible says that we need to present ourselves before the Lord with thanksgiving (Psalm 95:2). Many believers don't know how to pray and as the Bible says, you do not have because you do not ask. The key is knowing when we are to make petitions and when we should remain silent before the presence of the Lord to listen to His sweet voice. Many of us don't realize the power there is in thanksgiving rather than coming directly into the presence of our Father with some kind of request or need. Now imagine if your child came straight to you after you haven't seen him in days and asked for something. How bad would you feel, deep inside, knowing that as a parent you are to help your child, but at the same time, you feel like not meeting the request because of the ungrateful behavior that this child is manifesting. They may not mean to hurt your feelings, but because the world around them is made of that fabric, they think it is okay to keep asking and not be grateful. How many times have you, as a parent, felt like your child has been ungrateful when you buy something that is not to their liking, and sometimes they even throw a tantrum because they didn't get what they wanted? How many times have you felt the pain of feeling no gratitude coming from your child and all you are doing is for their best? Unfortunately, we live in a world where even our children are surrounded by the materialism and ungratefulness of this present age. Now allow me to say, there is no difference in the pain you feel from the pain your heavenly Father experiences when you, as a child of God, come into His presence and behave in the same manner. How many of us have done this before? Where we forget that our God before being our Lord, is actually our Father. How many times have we made the mistake of praying to God as if He is thousands of miles away in the universe and wondering if He is listening to us? How many times have we come into His presence and vented all of our frustrations or pulled out a list of prayer points, ignoring the very presence of the Holy Spirit? We can easily miss the presence of the Lord when we have a ritualistic approach to prayer, seeking answers to our prayers rather than His presence. How many times have you gone to a conference and expected to receive some kind of outstanding prophetic word, but instead of worshiping during the praise and worship time, you were too busy looking around or being distracted by your latest update on Facebook or your emails? How many times has God showed up and we have missed Him because we were too busy and anxious, thinking about our problems and praying for the same things over and over, when God is expecting for us to just trust Him and enjoy His presence. Being grateful is not part of our human nature and many of us struggle with this right through our lives. There are times when we are expected to be grateful but we simply don't know how to step into that realm. The only one who can show us how to be grateful at all times is the Holy Spirit. Being grateful is a kingdom principle that one must embrace and learn as part of our walk with the Lord. It may not come naturally, but as you keep thanking the Lord and seeking His face, you will be amazed how much your prayer life will change the moment you stop putting so much emphasis on your troubles, but instead, investing more of your time seeking Him and waiting on Him to meet with you. I can assure you that if you decide to pursue God, your prayer life will be revolutionized!

About Author

A lejandro Arias was born in San Jose, Costa Rica in 1987. At the age of seven he gave his heart to the Lord, following his mother's conversion. Just months later their faith would be severely tested, when it was discovered that Alejandro had a cancerous tumor lodged between his heart and lungs. Convinced that God had a destiny for his life in spite of the circumstances, he began to pray each day, believing God for his healing. When Alejandro was re-examined three months later, the doctors found that the tumor had miraculously disappeared.

Following his supernatural encounter with the power of God, Alejandro received the baptism of the Holy Spirit and began to develop a passion for passing out tracts and sharing the gospel. A Venezuelan missionary called Orlando Lopez saw the call of God on the young boy's life and began to mentor him, giving him opportunities to preach to hundreds at evangelistic outreaches in a local park. In 1999, Orlando felt led to take Alejandro with him to Venezuela to preach at evangelistic crusades. Many salvations and healings resulted.

Alejandro then began to preach and travel all over his native Costa Rica, covering almost the entire country with the gospel over the course of two years. At this time he also began to visit surrounding Latin American countries, such as Nicaragua, Guatemala and Colombia.

In 2002, Alejandro sensed the Lord calling him to make the United States home. AAIM continued to expand after the move, with opportunities arising to minister in countries such as Zimbabwe, Indonesia, Spain, Chile, Finland and Italy and others.

While in Lakeland, Florida in 2007, Alejandro saw a vision of the map of Australia and was prompted to travel to the island nation for the first time. This would be the first of many trips, one of which would see the Lord introducing him to his future wife, Rebekah.

In 2011 Alejandro and Rebekah were married in Perth, Australia among their friends and family. They travelled and ministered internationally for six months before returning to Australia to settle in Melbourne, Victoria.

Alejandro and Rebekah are blessed to see the doors that God is opening in USA, Australia and in previously unvisited nations. This is an exciting season and they can't wait to see what God has in store for the future! Alejandro and Rebekah are the proud parents of a beautiful girl named Carielle Lee Arias. Last December 2015, they both felt the call of God to move to the United States.

Currently they attend Sojourn Church in Dallas Texas. Alejandro is currently a credentialed minister with Victory Life International.

For more information about Alejandro Arias
or to order more books, contact:

AAIM Ministries (USA)
1849 Tiburon Bend
Lewisville TX, 75067
www.alejandroarias.org

AAIM (Australia)
7 Kingston Heath Ct
Connolly,WA 6038
www.alejandroarias.org

Made in the USA
Columbia, SC
01 June 2021